The Angel the Witch & the Warrior

The Angel Warrior Series

The Angel, the Witch & the Warrior - Book 1

Saving the World from my Bathtub - Book 2

The Princess & the Pink Moon Leeches - Book 3

The Avatar & the Crystal Key - Book 4

THE ANGEL
—— THE WITCH & ——
THE WARRIOR

21st Century Mind Body & Soul Refinement
Janine Regan-Sinclair

Printed in the United States of America.

Published by BookWhirl.com Publishing 11/08/12
PO Box 9031, Green Bay
WI 54308-9031, USA
www.BookWhirl.com

© 2012 Janine Regan-Sinclair. All rights reserved.

ISBN 13:   Softcover 978-1-61856-116-9
Kindle 978-1-61856-133-6
Adobe PDF 978-1-61856-134-3
ePub 978-1-61856-135-0

No part of this book may be reproduced, stored in a retrieval system or database, or transmitted in any form or by any means, electronic, mechanical, photo copying, recording or otherwise, without the prior permission of the author.

It is currently the law that authors and publishers must publish a disclaimer regarding the advice given in books relating to complementary therapies. As a complementary therapy practitioner I am not allowed to make any claims as to the effectiveness of exercises or treatments referred to in this book. By carrying out the exercises you resume full responsibility.

Therefore the information and exercises given are intended as a guide only. Neither the author nor publisher can accept any responsibility for any effects resulting from any exercise or treatment included in this book. All exercises must be carried out exactly as per the instructions given and are practiced at your own risk.

The information in this book is not a substitute for professional health care and readers are advised to see a medical practitioner in the case of illness.

Originally published in 2008 by Crystal Ki Press—ISBN: 978-0-9559745-0-2

Profits from this series of books will be donated to
The Crystal Ki Foundation
Visit www.thecrystalkifoundation.com

The Angel, the Witch & the Warrior

This book is dedicated to my father, brother, sister and nephew who are no longer with us but have been guiding me in spirit and a special thank you to my friends who encouraged me to share my truth . . . Thank you, I love you xx

Contents

1. Introduction 1
2. Why the Angel, the Witch and the Warrior? 7
3. Empaths 8
4. Complementary/Alternative Therapy 9
5. Exercise can be healing 13
6. Positive Emotions 13
7. Heal Thyself 16
8. How I Became a Practitioner 19
9. Sri Lanka 24
10. Karma 30
11. Science and Karma 33
12. The Bigger Picture 37
13. Dimensions—Physical and Non-Physical 41
14. Angels and Ascended Masters 44
15. New Energies and Transitional Problems 46
16. Atlantis, DNA and Indigo Children 48
17. Autistic Spectrum Disorders 49
18. The Conscious and the Sub-Conscious Mind 51
19. The Mass Consciousness creates our World 53
20. The Map of Consciousness 59
21. Mental and Emotional Causes of Disease 62
22. Disease and Cell Memory 67
23. Fear 69
24. Forgive them for you, not them! 73
25. The Chakras and Auric Bodies 75
26. Connecting to your Higher Self 88
27. Crystal Ki Healing Exercises 90
28. Meditation and Brainwaves 101
29. Ancestral Healing 109
30. Animal Medicines 110

31. Akashic Records: Breaking Vows, Pacts, Contracts or Agreements 114
32. Journey Work...115
33. Crystal Ki Healing—Case Studies and Soul Retrieval 117
34. Soul Purpose 124
35. 3rd Dimensional Signs..126
36. Television and Radio 131
37. Developing Spiritual Growth...133
38. Divine Truth and Prayer 135
39. Universal Spiritual Laws 137
40. Seed Atoms, Life and Death 142
41. Summary..146
42. Bibliography...148

Introduction

Have you ever wondered what it's all about? Life I mean. Does the same thing seem to happen to you over and over again? Does bad luck or good luck follow you around? Are your relationships a recipe for disaster, or do they run smoothly? When you stop and take a look you will begin to see a chain reaction of people, places, events and feelings, all being reflected in the magical illusion we call reality. Do you want to change your life for the better? If you do, here is your chance. This book will reward those with an open mind.

This book is for those who want to find out more about the bigger picture, spiritual growth and healing. It will teach you how to keep your personal energy clear, as well as the energy in your home. The tie cutting and energy clearing technique described later in this book are the most important exercises I have ever learnt; I use them every day.

Some of the events I have written about are ones that I have experienced and learnt from; some are other people's experiences, but the lessons are there nevertheless. Life, and its ups and downs, gets easier when you have looked at the bigger picture and understand the way it works.

I have spent many years researching and working with complementary healing techniques in search of some answers to the meaning of life and the pursuit of happiness. I have discovered that self-healing plays a big part of it. My goal is to help others find the inner peace and wellness that I now have, and to raise global healing awareness, because by healing ourselves, we will heal the planet.

I am sharing the information that has helped me towards enlightenment with all who care to take a look at themselves and make positive changes, healing mind and body. This knowledge is also for those who want to integrate and refine the soul through self-purification, working towards the ascension of the planet.

Please note that I have used the word negative in this book in regard to certain energies; it is a general word to describe low frequency energy, disharmony, dark energy, impurities and imbalance. There is no such thing as negative energy as it all comes from God. The whole point is to remove the imbalance and fill the gaps with balance and one word describes all.

I had been procrastinating for at least four years since I first had the idea for this book. I lacked the motivation to put it all on paper until I was given a digital Dictaphone, which helped make it happen.

I really didn't think of myself as a writer—until inspiration for the second book in the series arrived. *"Saving the World from my Bathtub,"* is about a healer who goes out of body when she is in the bath and travels to other worlds and dimensions, deporting aliens from this planet and co-creating with Source and the Galactic Federation. Her task is to cleanse the planet and the local Universe of low frequency energies and Beings, in the pursuit of global healing and creating the perfect world.

My intention in this book is to offer lots of different topics related to spiritual development, in order for you to investigate further the ones that interest you. It is meant to be a taster session of information that may help you lead happier, healthier lives, and, if you wish, to become enlightened through self-refinement and meditation. I hope you will find that every chapter has something interesting. I have tried to pack it with useful knowledge and guidance, from how to meditate, tie cutting and space clearing, the chakra system and journeying, to removing the seed fear of enlightenment, and activating DNA changes.

Some of the words in this book may come across as spiritual, but please don't let that put you off, as a lot of it is common sense when you think about it. Whether you are spiritual or not, I hope there will be something in the chapters ahead that will inspire you to further investigate whatever area you feel drawn to, and change your life forever, just as I did, together with many of my friends and family.

The answers are within you and all around you, if you decide to take a look, using whatever means you feel necessary. The most helpful way to find answers that I have found so far is by practising meditation. All you need to know will become clear, but you need to do some reading to help you get there, and to take time out to reflect on what you are learning.

I was born in Warwickshire in England, the youngest of five children, to working class Catholic parents. However, I stopped going to church when I was a teenager, deciding that I did not agree with the teachings of the church. I thought I would be okay if I was a good person and tried not to hurt anyone. I had been taught that God would forgive you if you were sorry for your sins, and that was all I needed to know at the time. I was thirteen and happy to believe that, but something deep inside me *knew* there was more to life than the solid things you can see and touch. There had to be! The phrase *'As you sow, so shall you reap'* was firmly imprinted on my young mind, even though, at the time, I was not fully sure what it meant.

I was a clairvoyant child who could see and talk to the little people in my garden, until the age of eleven when I decided to shut it down because I wanted to be like other girls at school. My school report read 'Janine is a pleasant and helpful girl but she lacks concentration', mainly because I was staring up at the sky wondering which planet I came from. Not this one for sure!

At seventeen years of age I found a job as a trainee draughtsperson in an architect's office and went to college to learn building studies. I stayed in the building industry until I was thirty-six, and could stand it no longer. This was when my father died and I was at an all-time low. I was unhappy and felt trapped in a 17-year relationship I no longer wanted to be in, and with a job I dreaded daily. I began to have panic attacks, and that was the beginning of big changes in my life. The panic attacks turned out to be an energetic entity (a low frequency energy mass) in my heart chakra that was making my hear palpitate; once it was removed I was fine. It must have entered when I was grieving.

On my 37th birthday I went to see a solicitor, and soon after took my son and a couple of suitcases and moved out of the family home. My sister very kindly let us move in with her, and we stayed for a year. During that time my digestive system and bladder just stopped functioning and I was admitted to hospital for over two weeks. Knowing what I do now, I believe that I could not stomach any more unhappiness or stress and my body was shutting down. It took me four months to get well, and this included some healing from a friend during that time. Intrigued, it was soon after my recovery that I attended my first healing workshop, and began my training as a practitioner.

My health began to improve, and I continued studying and training. I became a volunteer in the oncology department of a local hospital, where I spoke to outpatients about the benefits of complementary therapy. I began to work and teach in a complementary health clinic.

Some time later, and after becoming a master teacher, I channelled and developed my own system of healing and copyrighted it in 2005; it is called Crystal Ki Healing. This is a high vibration energy that includes opalescent diamond energy, the universal resonance frequency, and the keys to perfection. It involves passing discs and nets through the body and aura and can also be used to clear, for example, the body, animals, food, water, land and even the planet.

It was in 2006 during a healing treatment from three of my students, that I had what I believed to be my first conversation with God and my life changed forever. As they were working on me, I entered another dimension. The space I was in turned darker than the normal grey misty vision you get when you close your eyes. I was aware of a ladder leading to a trapdoor above me. I climbed the ladder and opened the door. All of a sudden, it became bright; white light was everywhere as if I had put my head up into a loft space that was painted brilliant white and never ending. There were no edges, no walls and a deep but gentle voice said, "You made it then?"

I knew instinctively it was my Creator and for a moment I thought I must have died. I panicked and replied, "Yes, but I'm not stopping" and quickly closed the trapdoor and descended. Meantime the girls were still working on me. I decided not to tell them, in case they thought I was crazy. My connection to Source has been very strong ever since, once I stopped questioning my sanity, of course!

My path has been a struggle at times and like many light workers I have been short of money. I made a major breakthrough in 2012 and it is so important, I have decided to share it. I was on the verge of giving up my spiritual work as I was not making enough money to live, when I discovered that my financial issues were due to a past life false belief buried deep in my aura and sub-consciousness. My belief was that God and the Universe did not love and support me, and guess what? This belief manifested; they couldn't support me because the belief created blocks. I would attract clients but they would cancel on me, students would not turn up for courses and so on. My situation got so bad, I even considered bankruptcy. But, thankfully, I found the false belief and removed it and things turned around within a week, once the false belief was gone.

I also had problems with being psychically attacked, even though I was not sending out any negativity at all, so I didn't understand why. Then a friend of mine introduced me to Bio-Physics and NES Health. This computer program gives you a top-to-toe print-out of your energetic health, and mine showed up a 'Fear of Attack'. I was surprised at this because I am a really courageous person and I always have been. Then I realised that this was deep-rooted again, and from my past, so it was on a deep sub-conscious level. I know I have been in wars and battles in past lives and therefore will have been subjected to attack and been fearful. It's obvious when I think about it. I removed this belief and the attacks stopped.

As we move into an era of interdimensional travel and extraterrestrial contact, it is really important to remove one's fears about other life forms, as these fears create your reality. A belief is a belief, only if you believe it! For example, if you believe extraterrestrials are bad, then you will create a reality that has bad ones in it. Let's face it, the media has certainly given us plenty of negative food for thought over the years, with movies about alien invasions and so on. I believe most of these beings are our friends and want to come and help us to evolve.

Of course, as with anything spiritual, it is wise to be discerning, but in order to manifest an intergalactic universe of love and peace, it's time to remove our fears and seek the divine truth: we are all one, we are all God's children and it's about time we behaved like we are!

As a teacher, I have come across many people who feel they are being attacked, and it will be because of their internal fear of attack on a subconscious level. I used the following exercise on myself to clear my fear of attack. It may help you too.

I asked my higher self to take my book entitled 'Fear of Attack' and put it on a bookshelf. I visualised this in my mind and then selected the book from the shelf and threw it into a white flame to purify it.

Then, because the body and internal organs can hold fears and beliefs, I visualised my body, and on a piece of white paper in my mind, I asked my higher self to show me the areas that needed 'fear of attack' clearing from them. I imagined rubbing out any 'shading' in these areas with an eraser, then colouring in these areas with a magic pen containing an appropriate colour. For me it was the colour gold.

Finally, I cleared any residual energy from my body and auric layers using a Crystal Ki disc and net. The Crystal Ki healing technique is in the back of this book and available as an audio download on my website www.crystalki.com

Since then, I have gone from strength to strength and feel like everybody is coming forward to help me and to donate money to my charity, The Crystal Ki Foundation.

I am currently starting up another venture to help rebalance the minds and bodies of young offenders and prisoners with my revolutionary 21 Day Mind Detox treatment. For more information visit: www.thecrystalkifoundation.com.

The 21 Day Mind Detox is a revolutionary treatment, developed in 2010, that cleanses the mind, body and spirit on every level. I incorporate my energy practitioner knowledge, with my spiritual abilities and my hypnotherapy skills to remove problematic imbalances that cause illness, stress and dis-ease. The imbalances are removed from the entire energy field of the person, from the cellular molecular to the auric layers. The subconscious mind is also cleansed, removing causes of dis-ease such as fears and phobias, addictions, Obsessive Compulsive Disorders (OCDs), serious illnesses, eating disorders and much more.

Treatment is generally completed in an initial session of between ninety minutes to two hours, followed by twenty-one remote healing sessions carried out at night while the client is asleep. Business or financial problems may also be improved as energetic blocks and limiting beliefs are gently removed. This treatment also aids soul refinement, as the vibrational frequency of the client is greatly improved as a result of the treatment.

Let's move now to the information I have gathered and would ask you to consider. The following chapters touch on theories and beliefs from many different and varied sources, and some very wise people I have had the privilege to come to know along my life's path, especially my parents and my many good friends.

I hope you enjoy reading it and it helps you on your journey.

2. Why the Angel, the Witch and the Warrior?

This title was chosen with reference to me, some of my previous lives and my present purpose as a warrior of light, teaching global healing awareness. Some years ago I learned how to journey through the different realms of existence through meditation.

During one journey very early on in my awakening, I could see myself from three different perspectives all at once—as a young woman being made to walk the plank on an old ship and looking down on to deep dark waters; I was to be drowned as a witch as I fell to my death. I could sense myself feeling at peace as I sank into the dark waters. I was also viewing this as an observer from above as a bird, and also as a sea creature in the depths of the sea. The death I saw was in the fourteenth century and I knew in my heart, back then I had been a white witch who healed people using herbs and potions. However I was not a real witch, if there is such a thing. I was a healer, and I was being murdered for my work, drowned at sea, terrifying and cruel beyond words. This was the beginning of being able to see past, present and future events with my mind's third-eye. Precognitive dreams and visions were to become common in my life.

Later, a journey took me underground to experience a shamanic healing, the death of a Shaman as it is called. I could see myself being pecked to death by a large flock of birds. This sounds traumatic but what happened next was a beautiful transformation. I could see this beautiful white angel rise from the dead body in triumph, a re-birth, like the phoenix from the ashes. I had shed my old fear and transcended to a new level of consciousness. This angelic being was pure of heart and resides within me to this day; hence the Angel in the title.

I have seen many of my lives, some good, some bad. I have been raped in a past life, which explains why I felt vulnerable in dresses in this life. I have also seen myself leading a troop of men on horseback into battle, and that warrior spirit is with me today as well.

I realise and understand that I can release the old parts of my personality and can rest easily in my 'I Am Presence,' my higher self having guided me home. The pain I used to feel has gone, and I feel clean and clear.

I am still working on my ascension process but I have cleared much trauma from my body on many levels. More recently my transformation was from a butterfly into a clear being of light, just like a diamond 'Crystal Ki.'

I have been a witch, an angel and a warrior. Now "I Am".

3. Empaths

I have chosen to talk about empaths first, as I am one myself. Many empathic people become healers or therapists. Being empathic (clairsentient) means that they feel or sense other people's emotions whereas telepathic people sense other people's thoughts. Being an empathic therapist can be very useful when working with clients but it can also be draining if you do not know how to stop picking up on the energy of others. If you are an empath it is important to set specific intentions and to protect your energy field. You may need to learn how to clear your energy field and place a protective shield around you to stop you from absorbing other people's negative energy.

I find it hard to be in certain places for too long, with supermarkets being one of the worst. I remember one instance of being in a supermarket and being overwhelmed with a tight feeling in my chest and feeling panic. I knew it wasn't my own emotions and when I turned to the next aisle, there was a lady having an anxiety attack, which I was feeling too. It was terrible. I had to get home quickly and clear myself, using the energy clearing techniques explained in this book. It is my intention to teach these techniques to as many people as possible, especially other therapists, as they are very adaptable, clearing negative energy from people, property and even the planet.

When I was younger I used to feel energy around me and I could get very distressed at times, and at thirteen I thought I was suffering from depression. I now know I was picking up on the sadness and grief that my mother was feeling at the time, after the loss of one of her siblings. She was one of sixteen children, and now at the age of 88, she only has one brother still alive, so all of those deaths must have been heartbreaking for her.

My mother is the only person I know who would refer to people as souls, and she would say things like "poor wee soul" when someone was ill or had died ('wee' in this context is from her Scottish ancestry). She is an amazing woman who worked hard all of her life and who retired at 76, under duress, due to health reasons. I honour her for the love and strength she has given me. She is an Angel and so was my father. I still miss him so much.

My empathic feelings are useful to me when I am working, as I can often sense how a client is feeling without having to ask them. When I do not want to pick up the energies or vibrations from other people, I set the intention that I am a divine channel for divine energy only, and that nothing will stick to me. I just think it and it is done. That way I protect my energy, and need my aura to be Teflon-coated too. It's non-stick, so to speak.

4. *Complementary/Alternative Therapy*

Due to the increasing use of complementary and alternative therapies these days, most of us have either tried, or know someone who has used, some sort of natural remedy. Whilst most developing countries work with traditional folk remedies, some surveys have shown that 35% to 50% of people in the affluent West, where modern medical health care is readily available, are happy to use more traditional therapies and techniques dating back to ancient Egypt and beyond.

The medical profession has begun to take complementary therapies more seriously, even allowing some of them to be used in hospital alongside modern medical care. The more holistic approach is widely recognised as being a better way to achieve optimum health and wellbeing. It is clear that health is directly affected not only by the person's physiological condition but also by the social, psychological, environmental and even spiritual aspects of their life, all of which contribute to a happy and healthy individual.

At last we have doctors and nurses who understand this and are training in complementary therapies as well as their medical studies. Physicians and medicines tend to only treat the physical symptoms; complementary therapies include the mental, emotional and spiritual causes of the physical symptoms. It is the cause that needs to be identified and eliminated, to stop the dis-ease returning.

A combination of medical and complementary approaches seems to work well with most problems. Some conditions, such as chronic fatigue, cannot be cured with medical procedures, yet positive results can be achieved with complementary therapies.

I once treated a lady who had been on sickness benefit for ten years because of chronic fatigue. I used Crystal Ki, and she was better after only three treatments. I found a huge dark cloud in the mental layer of her aura, removed it and filled the gaps with light. I'm sure you have heard the saying, *"I feel like I have a dark cloud hanging over me"*. Well that is exactly what had caused her illness and influenced her thoughts, making her feel depressed and mentally drained, which in turn lowered her energy levels. Who knows how much money had been spent on benefits over this period, when a different approach could have quickly eliminated the problem?

Many people give their power away to modern medicine, instead of eating healthily and having a more balanced approach regarding the mental, emotional and spiritual needs of their souls. To find a permanent solution or cure it is the root cause of the disease that needs to be removed, otherwise people are left with miasms and the illnesses re-occur.

Miasms have been described as the underlying causes for many known diseases. If symptoms are suppressed by medication, the root cause of the illness goes deeper into the body on both a physical and energetic level, and can manifest as dis-ease in the internal organs. Holistic therapies' aim is to identify and remove the root cause of the illness and to rebalance the energy centres, meridians, and so on. The emphasis is on being in touch with all aspects of the psyche and self care, dealing with emotional issues and expressing the emotions wisely.

For example, someone who eats good quality food, exercises daily and leads a fairly balanced lifestyle but bottles up their emotions, will store negative energy in one or more of the organs in their physical body, causing blocks in the energetic flow of their essential life force, potentially leading to illness and dis-ease. Some energies are not serious, but others can be, and can even be life-threatening. Holistic healthcare encourages people to have a good diet, exercise regularly and to release mental and emotional issues instead of suppressing them. It also promotes spiritual health awareness, using techniques such as meditation or gentle martial arts.

As we evolve as a species, we need to feed our spirit as well as our body, by doing some form of meditation or connecting with nature. All aspects of the psyche must be given adequate attention in order to maintain balance and optimum health within the whole body. Psychoneuroimmunology (mind/body medicine) is the field of science that states that health of mind as well as body are both essential, as they are intimately related, and affected by each other.

As the Mother Earth changes her vibration and we ascend to higher levels of consciousness, it is essential that we care for our minds and bodies in whatever ways are suited to our individual essence. We all respond better to certain treatments rather than others, and searching for the right one for you is important. Please try two or three other therapies, if the first one does not work for you. I have tried many, with my favourite being massage with the emphasis on acupressure points in the body. I feel like I am floating after a good massage. I have tried Bowen therapy, reflexology, kinesiology, Crystal Ki, acupuncture, homeopathy, flower formulas and chiropractic treatments. I can recommend all of them, they all worked for me.

You may choose to check out the reputation of the practitioner by asking around. You can ask the universe to guide you to a competent practitioner. You will get help if you ask. Anything you hear or see three times is a message from the cosmos and is sent to guide you, so be alert.

I have heard sceptics say that natural, or complementary therapies cause the 'placebo effect.' A placebo is a neutral, chemically inactive substance, like a sugar pill, that is used in medical trials as a control against which the effectiveness of new drugs can be measured. However, patients given a placebo, often display improvements to their condition that are not attributable to a drug or other medical procedure. This is the so-called 'placebo effect.'

I remember watching a documentary where fake operations were carried out to see whether it was possible to induce a placebo effect. In one case, where a man had a damaged knee, the surgeons made an incision, and then sewed the skin back up, to make it look like corrective surgery had taken place, leaving the man with his knee still damaged. However, after the surgery the knee problem improved. Why? Because the patient did not know he had received a fake operation. As far as he knew, he had been given an anaesthetic, which put him out for a while, and when he woke he clearly had a scar, and that was enough to convince his mind that the body had been repaired. Due to the power of his mind over his body, the knee repaired itself.

Research by the makers of the documentary revealed that placebos have a positive effect on 30% to 90% of the people in trials. My point is that whilst some results that come from complementary therapy may be the result of a placebo effect—and that is to be applauded, as a positive result is the goal no matter how it is achieved—most positive results are not due to the placebo effect. They are the result of a re-balancing of the energetic bodies.

5. Exercise can be healing

There are many ways to keep healthy, and exercise is very popular. For example swimming helps you to feel supported by the divine, it is good for your chakras and you can set your intention so that the water will cleanse you on all levels before you swim, thus enhancing the experience. Intentions are extremely powerful, as I will explain later.

Walking in nature is excellent for all ages as it helps to align the chakras and enhance energetic flow. Walking helps with spiritual and physical integration, and if you are walking outside in the park or in the woods it helps to remove energy blocks, clears the lungs and any energetic 'cobwebs'. Walking barefoot encourages adrenalin levels to drop and induces relaxation. It is also very grounding.

Body building helps to gain strength for challenges that we may face along our path, and is excellent for all chakras as a strong body evokes a strong mind.

Martial arts are all good forms of exercise and help balance the chakras, especially the higher ones, and are excellent for spiritual growth and discipline.

Any exercise is beneficial to your mind, body and soul, and it is important that you exercise on a regular basis, to keep yourself balanced in all areas.

6. Positive Emotions

Research has shown that positive people are healthier than negative, pessimistic types. Emotions such as hope and joy are powerful and produce self-healing when positive thinking interacts with diet and exercise.

Emotional support is essential, and relationships are a vital part of leading a happy, optimistic life blessed with good health. Isolated people have more health problems, as it is difficult to have a rich emotional life when you are alone.

Having a sense of humour helps too; people who laugh a lot tend to suffer less with dis-harmony related to stress, fatigue, tension and depression. Laughter eases tensions in the muscles and makes us breathe deeply, which is good for the circulation and releases endorphins into the system. Laughter is the body's natural pain relieving opiate. Mirth is a great healer, so my advice is to start laughing and then laugh some more. Laughter dissipates negative energy. When you feel good, life is a breeze, and being happy is achievable even when you are ill. You will get better quicker if you laugh a lot.

A positive person will see the glass as half-full, whilst the negative person will see it as half empty. The half-full view will lead to better health and will create a more positive experience in the 3D reality that we inhabit. Your thoughts, and especially your emotions, create your reality, or at least your perception of reality. If you are a negative, pessimistic person but are not suffering from depression, you could self-help by changing your perspective, thinking more positively and taking control of your thoughts. Instead of seeing yourself, perhaps, as a failure, turn it around and see yourself as a success for 'having a go' in the first place. If you have depression, you will need some help, either complementary or medical. I see a dark cloud in the aura of clients who are depressed. This is easily removed in one treatment or even using distant healing.

Every problem has a solution, and by stopping and breathing deeply when confronted with a problem, you allow divine input from a higher source to guide you towards the solution. We fall over in order to learn how to pick ourselves up. That's life, it is cyclical, full of peaks and troughs; we need to know and accept that and to go with the flow. All learning situations are positive, so don't beat yourself up when you make a mistake; give yourself a pat on the back for trying. Dust yourself down and have another go.

Practices like meditation and yoga all help to focus your thoughts and calm the mind and body. Learning to take control of your mind can change your thoughts. Next time you start to think negative thoughts, stop yourself and consciously think of something you love, or bring a happy memory to mind. This way you are taking control. Your mind is the slave, you are the master. If you allow it to run wild, thinking rubbish, it will. Learning to control your thoughts will lead you to the emotional feelings that are the creational power behind your reality. Balancing your mind and body will lead to peaceful, emotional wellbeing. This will change your life.

Balance is very important. You are unbalanced if you only give attention to the nice parts of yourself, and if you ignore the dark side of yourself then the energy will eventually explode like a time bomb. Even if you appear to feel centred and grounded, you are probably heading for trouble.

These pent-up emotions must escape eventually, and when repressed emotions surface it can be a nasty sight. If you feel angry, release it, stamp your feet, shout out, cry, do whatever it takes to get it out because if you don't you may suffer as a result. All emotions are there for a reason, they need to be addressed and worked through, not ignored or pushed aside.

I found the following exercise useful when I needed to release old emotional baggage. It is called 'Self Identity, through Ho'oponopono' and was developed by Morrnah Nalamaku Simeona; it is taught now by Ihaleakala Hew Len, Ph.D.

First, set the intention that the purpose of this exercise is to help release any old emotional energy that is not for your highest good. Then repeat the following phrases over and over for at least five to ten minutes or even longer, until it stirs your emotions and brings them to the surface. The version below includes two extra lines, identified in italics. I have found adding these gives a more powerful healing effect:

I Love You
I'm Sorry
Please Forgive Me
Thank You
I Forgive You
I Forgive Me

Repeating these simple but powerful words may bring to mind a person you are in conflict with or an incident that troubled you. At this point you may be moved to tears, and the tears are the important part, as that is the natural emotional release mechanism in the human body. We have tear ducts in order to cry and release stress. Crying is essential to releasing and letting go, which is vital to the healing process.

The next exercise involves writing a letter to the person with whom you are in conflict, or about the incident that has upset you. First, find somewhere peaceful and set aside some time alone, and then write a letter, pouring out all of your pent-up emotions and thoughts onto the paper. This releases the energy from your system as soon as you start to write. It is important not to read the letter again once you have written it. Once you have finished, take the letter outside and burn it. This transmutes the energy and purifies it. It may take a few sessions before you are ready to let go and forgive, but this method can work wonders.

I once wrote a letter that took me six hours of stopping and starting, as I cried like a baby all of the way through. I felt exhausted but a couple of days later I felt so happy and clear. I just knew that I had forgiven the people involved and had let go of the issues I had written about.

The best thing about these exercises is that they are free and anyone can try them. They really work. I know through experience.

7. Heal Thyself

It had been six years since the death of my father and only two months since the death of my brother at Christmas in 2006. It was now February 2007 and I had the first recall on my Pap (smear) test; they said I had pre-cancerous cells on my cervix. I sought deep within me and knew that this was caused by repressed emotional baggage. A few good emotional crying sessions, I hoped, would help to release it, allowing me to feel at peace, and actually I felt quite positive about the results; I had never really found it easy to cry. Over the next few weeks, I had gone to Sri-Lanka on a spiritual holiday, had met a new man, moved house and then experienced the tragic death of my brother's son, who was murdered. Well, let's just say that with all of this going on, it meant that I forgot all about that smear test.

Two months after my nephew's death, I was recalled for more tests, the results of which returned with pre-cancerous cells present. All of this in just six months—it was all too much. This time, however, they wanted me to go to the hospital for a colposcopy— *"no way are they going to be cutting into me"* I thought, and I refused the treatment. I told only two people, friends who were both first-class therapists, both medically and holistically trained, who said that they would help me if I needed them. I had all the skills needed to fix this. I did have a couple of treatments from them, but I did not work on myself until I kept hearing the word cancer, over and over. All right, I protested, I've got the message. I had tried to ignore it, but on reflection thought better of it and meditated on the issue by doing journey work (described in Chapter 32). I had read somewhere that it was possible to communicate with various aspects of the self, and asked questions of the four layers of my auric body and psyche, as I felt they could help. It worked. I found answers.

My higher self told me that the pre-cancerous cells would turn to cancer if I did not take action and start to work on eliminating them straight away; my physical body told me to only eat organic food and to cut out sugars, dairy, meat and bread.

During a treatment a therapist friend said that the problem was due to repressed toxic emotions that had been sent from my internal organs and had collected in my cervix. So, I knew what had caused it, but I needed to talk to my emotional body and find each situation individually and work on releasing the attached emotional issues, in order to heal them. Much of it was hurt, grief and anger accumulated over many lifetimes. Each day for three weeks, I would meditate, find an issue and deal with it, talking it through with the higher self of the person involved, forgiving them, letting it go, and filling the voids with healing light.

As I let go, I would also visualise the bad cells as blackberries on a bush, and see my angels take them away, a few at a time, ensuring that I dealt with each issue that was stored there. My mental body told me I was thinking too much and needed to retreat into myself for a while to concentrate on my healing process. I did spend a lot of time in my own head, and reading spiritual books, and doing preparatory work. My spiritual body said to raise my vibration by chanting, listening to classical music, and to meditate for peace and harmony within. My higher self had told me not to worry, that my soul had chosen for me to experience this so that I could heal myself and have more belief in my abilities as a healer, practitioner and teacher. I felt calm about the answers, and worked on myself with faith for those three weeks. Then one day my spirit guide, Peter, told me I could stop. It was clear; all negative emotional cell memories had gone. I felt a real sense of achievement.

I later called the surgery to book for another examination and to make sure all was well, but contracted a yeast infection and had to cancel my appointment. These infections were something I had experienced on and off since I was twenty years old. When I was thirty-one I had an operation where the surgeon removed a section of skin from my perineum in the hope that this would solve the problem, but it didn't. In fact, it just resulted in a nasty infection and made me ill for two weeks, with the problem returning some months later.

I was now forty-two and the same problem was back; time to deal with it again. I spoke to a homeopath at the clinic I worked in who said it was a miasm, and gave me four homeopathic opium pilules. She advised me to take one that evening and said that I would know when to take the rest.

Homeopathy perceives miasms as the underlying mental causes for many symptoms in the body. If illness and symptoms are suppressed by medication, the root cause can go deeper and can manifest as disease in the internal organs. Opium pilules can treat miasms, and my deep-rooted issues had caused very irritating yeast infections.

This was a deep-rooted disease, and I needed to look within myself to see where the cause of it lay, and with the help of my higher self, I was advised to take one pilule every three days and to meditate to find what had caused this ongoing condition in the first place. It wasn't too long before I could see the cause—my first love, who ended our relationship when I was twenty years old. It broke my heart, and was what had been causing the problem. I promptly did a tie cutting meditation, which healed the pain and soon afterwards the problem had gone. This shows that causes of disease are not always in the same place as the illness: my broken heart had caused the infection in my base chakra.

I was then able to go back to the surgery and have another smear test to check that no pre-cancerous cells were present. The results came back still showing a problem. This confused me for a short while, until a friend and I decided to meditate and find out why the result had not changed. We were told that I had had the re-test only six weeks after the treatment and I should have allowed the body eight to ten weeks to regenerate the cells. I also needed to work on removing the physical cells as well as the cell memory.

Another test at my local surgery showed the same result, which meant me having to have a colposcopy test anyway. I was then told that the results were a waste of time because six months are needed between tests and I had only waited three. The doctor should not have taken the tests so close together. I would have to wait for another six months before I could be re-tested.

Whilst I was waiting, I remembered hearing about a little boy who removed a tumour from his body using visualisation techniques. He sent a Pacman, like the one in computer games, into his body to eat the tumour a little piece at a time until it had gone. This seemed logical to me, and I decided to do the same, only the creature that came to my mind looked like a worm or a leech. I created this being in my mind and set the intention that it was going to remove the bad cells from my physical body, piece by piece, over a twenty-one day period. I had been told that people can be programmed or deprogrammed over a twenty-one day period, and that this intention was important as it was conditioning the energy of the treatment. I worked on myself each day for those three weeks until I could see in my mind's eye that the cells were gone. Then I visualised the leech leaving my body. This seemed to have cured the problem, but I would still need to have the medical test to make sure. This time, however, the result came back negative. I was clear.

8. How I Became a Practitioner

It was not really until the age of thirty-five and having experienced repeated stomach problems and continual infections and digestive problems that I became more aware of complementary therapies.

One friend was a healer who worked with energy and the chakras, and, after my father died, I decided to go for a treatment and was really impressed; I could not believe how much better I felt after an hour's treatment. It was not long after that that a group of my friends and I decided to learn how to do that too.

I was instantly hooked. There were a group of five of us and my energy seemed to flow differently; they all seemed to have hot hands when we were working, whereas I had cold hands, with cold energy flowing out of them. Needless to say my self-esteem went down and I knocked myself, thinking why am I so different, how come I have I got cold hands? It was only later I realised I was channelling different energies. They were all working with earth energies and I seemed to be working with a higher vibration, and that was reason for the difference in the temperature I could feel. The Crystal Ki energy is cool and looks like clear diamonds, with all of the colours of the rainbow in it.

So I studied to become a Master Teacher and attained that level quite quickly. Two to three years is the usual timescale to achieve this, but I am one of those people who when I find something I love doing, I tend to go full steam ahead. That is exactly the approach I have taken since, with my whole spiritual growth, learning different forms of complementary therapy and raising my conscious awareness at a spiritual level, on a path to seek the truth.

The truth I seek is the Divine Truth. This may differ to other peoples' understanding of truth, as we all see truth from our own perspective, depending on where we are in our journeys. However, in my view, there is only one Divine Truth!

Over the years I have come across people using a wide variety of therapeutic techniques, from Shamans to people who practise witchcraft. Whilst these were all very interesting experiences, their approaches were not for me or my energy at all.

I did learn a lot about psychic protection and how to retrieve energy that had been taken from me. I learned that having your energy stolen, or sleep paralysis, can be a form of psychic attack. It took me more than three years to find out that someone I trusted had been, either consciously or subconsciously, draining 50% of my energy, via an invisible psychic cord. We all have invisible psychic connections to one another, they are energetic ties; some are good and some are not. The negative ones need to be cut, as they can be used to control or drain us.

Cutting the bad ones is a speciality of mine. Cutting cords, cutting ties, cutting negative connections with people, places and even material items. It is amazing how much energy you can lose this way, and it is also amazing how many people are pullers, be it on your heartstrings through need, or through guilt, all sorts of things. I needed to be free of these ties, to be able to just Be, and it was therefore important that I learned how to cut them all.

I know we are all one on a spiritual level, but living in the third dimensional world, I craved solitude, and it has done me the world of good spending time alone. I have been slowly letting go of more and more people who were around me. Even though they were good people, with good intentions, it is fair to say some would have held me back if I had allowed them to.

Unfortunately the person who was draining my energy was one of those. I honour her spirit for the things that she taught me, but within a short period of time there was nothing more to learn from her and I became very despondent and disillusioned. Then I was fearful, because I considered her very wise and knowledgeable and a guiding light. I looked up to her, and I guess I put her on a pedestal, but at that time I was new to all this, and until I was in my late thirties I wasn't very spiritually aware. But psychic protection, using your mind's eye, or balancing chakras, and all of the things which are now part of my daily life, were something I barely knew about. At that time I only knew two people who practised these things.

Then when I woke up, that was it; it was like a light bulb was turned on in my head. I started to learn about meditation, healing and psychic protection. I realised that psychic attacks were mainly my own fault because I was having negative thoughts towards a particular person and that person psychically attacked me as a result.

In general, psychic attacks are a result of our energy being returned to us, but sometimes the shadow self of a person may be attacking, so that you can learn discernment and help you to see through their persona. If this is the case, the wise thing to do is to cut the ties.

The shadow self or dark side of our psyche is sometimes referred to as the enemy within. It is the part of us that has been created as a result of the choices we have made in our lives. Thomas Moore in 'The Care of the Soul' states that *"The person we choose to be, automatically creates the dark double, the person we choose not to be."*

The shadow self contains all of our repressed emotions and cravings, our ignored needs and shortcomings. If you were treated badly by someone, and repressed your anger and rage, those emotions become part of the shadow self, which over the years can become a destructive sub-personality if not confronted and healed.

For example, your choices could have been career-related—you became a solicitor to please your parents, when you really wanted to be an artist. The shadow contains both positive and negative, and there may be light in the shadow that can be salvaged through recognition and healing. The light within may prove to be a brilliant artist instead of a mediocre solicitor, proving that we should follow our heart's desires.

The shadow self will behave badly until it is given a voice and taken notice of. Usually the shadow demands attention as we hit mid-life, and this is when many people change their career, relationships or direction. It is more important than ever to heal this shadow self now, in order for us to ascend to higher levels of consciousness.

Most people see the shadow as negative and try to ignore it, only knowing themselves as persona, and that is all that they allow other people to see. The persona is the ego aspect that is presented to the world for approval. It is a kind of mask and is not always a true representation. A person who spends most of their time wearing this mask is out of balance, and, by ignoring the shadow, blocks not only communication in relationships, but also their personal and spiritual development.

The Angel, the Witch & the Warrior

The seeds for a happy future quite often lay within this rejected, repressed shadow self. On a psychic level, the darker side can cause people real harm and needs to be kept under control. The darker self can be manipulated by outside influences, and can actually psychically attack people, either with or without the person's knowledge. It can also be damaging to the self, and this aspect is referred to as the self-saboteur. The problem is that the person is responsible for their shadow self, and if it is attacking someone, they themselves are the one who receives the karmic consequences as a result.

The best way forward is to heal all aspects of this shadow, and in doing so the person's life will usually change for the better. There may be a repressed male or female side of the personality in the shadow, and as human beings are psychologically androgynous, it is important to tend to these parts of the psyche.

In the past these aspects were brought to our attention as we hit mid-life, but because of the planetary changes taking place, age is no longer an issue, and we can feel the need to seek healing and balance much sooner. Instigating these changes can be a form of re-birth into a completely new way of being. At the same time, it is also important to attend to our spiritual needs through some form of meditation, yoga or similar.

The inner child is also an important part of the human psyche that needs to be cared for and healed. The inner child resides within all adults as the part of us that loves to play and have fun. A child who was abused or ignored and not correctly nurtured may have inner child issues that form parts of the shadow self in later life.

Healing this inner child can be very emotional for the person concerned but it is well worth the effort, as wholeness and peace can be achieved. It is human nature to be nurtured and to nurture. Loving and praising a child can sculpt them into wonderful balanced adults and parents.

It is important to tend to all aspects of the self in order to be a well-balanced happy person. My inner child loves to walk along the beach with her feet in the sea collecting shells, and if she's lucky she finds something special like a starfish. On her last holiday she found three, which was quite significant at the time.

9. Sri Lanka

After Christmas was over in 2006, I had been getting a strong feeling that I needed to go to India or somewhere in Asia. I wanted a friend to come with me, but she could not get away until the summer due to studying for the finals of a master's degree she was taking. By now it was early April and I just decided I was going somewhere; anywhere spiritual would have been okay with me. I asked my Angels to help me find the right place, and within hours I was paying for a two week holiday in Sri Lanka, and I was going alone.

A couple of weeks later I was on my way. I had only travelled alone a few times before, and this was the furthest I had been, and I decided that it would be a spiritual adventure. The one thing that I specified to the Universe was that I wanted to meet a Buddhist Master.

When I arrived at my hotel, which at first glance looked good, I was rather jet-lagged and went straight to bed. The heat and humidity took time to get used to, but after a day or so I became acclimatised and re-energised.

The hotel was on a beach on the south-west coast and I was inspired to connect with the sea and go snorkelling. I quickly found a guide and was off on the roughest train ride I had ever had, to a village on the south coast about an hour away from where I was staying.

Compared to the trains in England I found the journey a great culture shock, but fun nevertheless. My Sri Lankan guide was called Serj. He introduced me to his friends, one of whom was a young Australian woman who had fallen in love with a Sri Lankan man and had been living with him for almost eighteen months. She was a lovely girl and I felt very comfortable with her, even though I was old enough to be her mother.

We ended up snorkelling together and the water was perfect, with amazing coral and beautiful puffer fish, and some electric blue fish I had only ever seen on the television. Being a Piscean I felt really at home and the couple of hours we spent in the sea, soon went by. After lunch, Serj took me to see where his family lived. The house had three bedrooms and was about five metres away from the main railway line. The bathroom was a concrete room with a hole in the floor, a cold tap with a hosepipe attached, with only a bucket to wash with. It was not quite a tin hut, but basic living would be an understatement. I knew they were on low wages, but compared to living standards back in England, this really was poverty.

Working a nine hour, six day week, Serj earned less in a month than I charged for one hour's consultation at the clinic back home. The whole experience was a real eye opener. When he took me back to the hotel I gave him a generous tip for being my guide for the day.

There were armed guards at the hotel gates, as had all the hotels; it made you feel safe and uneasy at the same time. Can you imagine armed guards at the entrance to every hotel in England? No way! It made me realise how lucky I was to have the level of freedom I take for granted back home.

The next day I decided to sit out by the pool and read my book. It was yet another beautiful day and the pool was very cooling. I befriended a couple from England who said that they had been told about a beautiful waterfall where visitors could go swimming in cold water, unlike the warm water in the pool. They were going later that afternoon and invited me along. I said yes, of course; the cold water was calling me.

We later met up with their guide Kalum, and went off in his tuk tuk, a three wheeled vehicle that was a cross between a bike and a car, sometimes called a cabin cycle and very popular in Asia. The seats are not very soft for long journeys, the roads were full of pot holes and the other drivers were a nightmare, not to mention the odd cow and chicken roaming around in the middle of the road; the journey was certainly an experience in itself.

When we arrived, we had to walk for ten to fifteen minutes to reach the waterfall through the woods. When we arrived, however, it was the most amazing oasis, just perfect. We had to cross to the other side of the stream over some stepping stones. I had come prepared wearing my swimsuit under my clothes; I took my trousers and shoes off and made my way to the other side of the stream. On the other side was a wall of stone and rocks approximately three or four metres high. Just beyond that was a beautiful waterfall about two metres wide and five metres high flowing into a pool about fifteen metres in diameter. The rocks had formed a shelf around the outside of one half of the pool, just below the water level. When you were tired, you could sit on the shelf in the water and rest. Kalum climbed to the top of the higher rocks; there you could look down into the crystal clear cold water of the pool below the waterfall. He dived in from the high rocks but I was not quite brave enough to try that. The water was fantastic, it was so cold just as promised, just what we needed to cool down. We swam for an hour or so and then made our way to a house that belonged to a friend of Kalum. Having worked up an appetite we ate some local cuisine before making our way back to the hotel.

I had decided that I was going to work on raising my vibration by cleansing my chakras and having plenty of massages while I was there. I meditated every day and in no time at all I could clearly see the Ascended Masters, Buddha, Jesus Christ, Lady Nada and Quan Yin, almost as soon as I closed my eyes, it was amazing. I was so peaceful and felt on top of the world.

Most days I would carry out some sort of cleansing on the land using light grids to clear Tsunami damage and sadness, with the help of these Ascended Masters. I now realised why I was here and not in India. There was so much sadness in the ground and in the atmosphere around Sri Lanka. It really needed cleansing.

The next trip I took was to a local turtle sanctuary. The locals collected the turtle eggs in a bid to keep them safe and protected. They kept them in tanks until they matured and could be released into the sea. Some of the turtles were amazing; one was an albino that liked very much to be tickled. I was lucky enough to hold her, she was beautiful and so friendly, and I felt really honoured to have held her, as albino turtles are rare. I was invited to come back later that evening and help release the turtles back into the sea, but I was unable to make it. Fond memories of that amazing little albino turtle I tickled still remain with me.

During my time in Sri Lanka the locals were celebrating the birthday of Buddha by bringing flowers to the temples and worshipping through prayer and meditation. One afternoon, the hotel manager had arranged transport to the local temple, which had a statue of Buddha that was twenty-five meters high, and this impressive, awesome sight could be seen from miles away. I decided to go along.

Before we went, however, I had an experience that I recall very strongly. You may remember that I had asked the Universe to ensure that during my trip I met a Buddhist Master. On this particular morning, a Buddhist monk had come to the hotel to give an hour's talk about life and peace. I was very excited and had woken up extra early in the morning, bathed, and dressed in white; I made my way to the conference room and managed to secure a front row seat.

By sitting at the front I was actually sitting within the monk's aura, which was an amazing aquamarine with patches of yellow; the Christ/Buddha consciousness colours. I could certainly feel the effect, which was blissful. The room was so peaceful you could have heard a pin drop when this wise soul opened his mouth to speak to us. I could have cried. I felt so humbled by his tone.

He spoke about peace, and that Buddhists do not speak of God but only of the Mind. This was fine with me, as I had understood for some time that WE ARE GOD, and that God is the collective consciousness of all of us; one mind so to speak. However I felt that his words might have shocked some of the people in the room. Many believe that we are individual souls and that God is a separate entity, the Supreme Soul. This is also a possibility. I don't think it really matters as long as we believe and behave accordingly, with God in our hearts.

The one point he stressed was that women should not feel the need to wear makeup, because they were beautiful enough without it. How right he was but the pressure placed on woman by modern society to look glamorous is so high. This meeting was one of the highlights of my trip, and I have never seen those colours around another human being to this day.

Before we left the hotel for our trip to the temple in the afternoon, the manager gave me a bag full of white flowers. The flowers were an offering to be placed on each of the different alters at the temple.

It was only a short drive to the temple and when we I arrived I washed the flowers in cold water, as was the tradition, and moved from one room to the next, placing the flowers as I had been directed, on the alter in front of each of the Buddha statues and then saying a brief prayer. The temple was huge and had lots of smaller holy buildings around the main arena. There must have been 10,000 people, all walking barefoot from room to room, washing the flowers they had brought with them to leave on the various alters. I was the only white person there and I felt like Hayley Mills in one of those old movies I would watch as a child with my father on a Sunday afternoon.

By the end of the day I was floating, having soaked up some of the monk's energy, and praying and meditating all afternoon; it couldn't get any better than this. I felt nothing but total inner peace.

The whole trip was pulling me more and more towards the Buddhist lifestyle. Their wonderful altruistic philosophy seemed to be the way to live. You could feel the peace when you were talking to a true Buddhist. They emanated calm. Not being religious and against being labelled, in the end I decided against becoming a Buddhist and to stick with my own union with Source, to just try and be the best person I could be, and to be free.

I had a new spiritual guide come to me on that trip. His name was Matthew, and that was all I knew about him until one evening when another lightworker, a beautiful woman in her thirties who was also clairvoyant told me she could see him. She said he was very important-looking, wearing a long white robe and that he was blowing me kisses, saying that he loved me.

I had another guide called Jupiter, a dolphin, a cheeky one at that, always smiling like he had not got a care in the world. Whenever I had to solve a problem, he was there to help. Jupiter asked me to place my hand on the back of the woman's heart and pass some information on to her. With her permission, I placed my hand on her back and she said that all that she could feel was unconditional love flowing through her heart. She could see the dolphin smiling and the connection was made. I felt she would see him again. Dolphins are amongst the wisest creatures on the planet and can teach us many things to help raise our frequency and help heal ourselves.

Another highlight of my holiday was a visit to the elephant orphanage, and my trip to the Temple of Tooth in Kandy, four hours north of Beruwela. It felt a lot longer than four hours on those bumpy roads, I can tell you. The guide Kalum had hired a mini-bus to take three of us on a two-day trip.

The temple was amazing; it was like a large white and gold palace. The outside walls were covered completely in tubes of light and it was so bright you could see it for miles. The inside was just as beautiful, with carved statues and gold everywhere. There was a large golden cask that was said to house the tooth of Buddha himself, but the queue to get near to it was very long, and we were short of time. I did get a glance though. It was all very impressive and a wonderful trip. I would recommend it.

I was allowed to bathe a full-grown female elephant—another fantastic experience. I can see why people want to work with these animals full-time; they are so loving and powerful. I was lucky enough to be able to get in the river with her and scrubbed her with a piece of coconut shell. She absolutely loved it. I could have stayed there all day. Afterwards I sat on her back and she got up and took me for a walk around the woodland. I was also able to feed her and tickle her tongue. For a short while I really felt connected to her and it almost felt as if we could read each other's minds. I had heard about people who use telepathy to communicate with animals and for a while thought I could do it too. I placed my hand on her forehead and the words *"I love you"* came into my head. Was it her, or me? I don't know. Something happened though, and on a much higher level of consciousness. Maybe our higher selves were communicating and we could feel the vibrations. It was a heartfelt moment, a universal gift.

I was so happy that day. These animals are so gentle and yet their power is phenomenal. I came back home a more content human being filled with peace and gratitude for the blessings in my life.

This trip was a turning point in my life and self-development, in that I moved on very quickly when I returned home. I bought a property the week after I came home, and met a new man as well. While I was away, I had made some notes for a book I was thinking of writing (this book), decided that I needed to stop procrastinating, and signed up for a book-writing course.

That was in April 2007. I have come a long way since then and achieved more than I thought I could. I feel a bliss surrounding me that I can almost taste, it is so sweet.

10. Karma

In order to understand life and how it works, it is important to know a little about karma. We are taught that we create karma with every thought, word and deed. All actions have a reaction, and they all have consequences to you, your family, people you interact with and your whole community, the whole world, and no one can escape it. Karma teaches us how to behave, and that 'what goes around, comes around'. In general, if you're good to people, people will be good to you. If they are not, maybe you are being tested.

Karma helps us to evolve spiritually into aspects of being connected with the higher self, allowing us to be more compassionate, sensitive and wise. The thing you need to watch out for is the ego. The ego self does not stop functioning when we are growing, and you can still find yourself relating to others from a selfish point of view. The ego needs to be conquered in order for us to progress.

What is karma?

There are basically four types:

- The first is the result of all past life actions—your total cosmic debt. This is added to, or reduced, by your actions on a daily basis.
- The second is the part of your past life karmic debt that has been worked on in this life. If you lessen your karmic debt in this life, you get to work on more of your past life debts and clear them —or not.

- The third is karma that is added to your past life karmic debt, based on your actions in this life. If you do not reduce your past life karmic debt and instead add more debt, karma will be sent to your future lives to be worked upon.
- The fourth is instant karma. It's created daily and is worked off immediately. It doesn't get added to past life karmic debt. For example, if you murder someone, you get sent to jail—debt paid!

Karma means *"As you sow, so shall you reap."* In other words, you get back what you give out, and this applies to all areas of life. It is about cause and effect; action and reaction; justice will be done. Your karma is your responsibility and there is no escaping it.

Next time something 'bad' happens to you, stop and think *"What did I do to bring this on?"* The answer will soon come. Remember that thoughts, words and deeds create karma; badmouthing someone or thinking nasty thoughts about them is actually a form of psychic attack. It will come back on you, guaranteed!

Somebody cuts you up in your car and you are tempted to swear and curse. I advise you to stop and think! You will be psychically attacking that person, creating bad karma for yourself. The wise thing to do would be to see it as a test. Just take a deep breath and let it go—test passed! If you are really wise, you might think, *"Bless them, they must be in a hurry."* When you bless someone, you are sending out very positive vibes and thus invoking positive karma for yourself upon its return. Simple!

This way of thinking teaches that life is a constant cycle of birth, death and reincarnation. It exists in order for us to learn. Earth is a beautiful mystery school containing the secrets of success. The answer is simple, and love is the key. We keep incarnating until we have learnt our lessons. It's all about spiritual growth and purification, and Karma exists solely in order for us to learn. It's not about punishment, although it can feel that way at times; your experience is exactly that, your experience—you created it. It's not just you; we are all in the same boat.

Before we incarnate (are born into this lifetime), we all agree to face certain trials and tribulations. These are the result of actions in our past lives, our cosmic debt. When we are born we have our past life memories erased. There are two reasons for this; one is to make sure we have really learnt our lessons from the past, and the other is to stop us from being overwhelmed by all that memory from all of those lives. Imagine all of that information consciously in your head; it doesn't bear thinking about.

The whole process is about evolving into higher levels of perfection, purifying every thought, word and deed. This applies to everybody, whether you are spiritual or not. There are no exceptions. It is universal justice for all; it is completely fair and accurate. There are no karmic mistakes. For example, there are no innocent people in prison. They might be innocent of the crime they are incarcerated for in this life, but it may be that they have committed a crime in a past life and got away with it. Or, so they thought. There is no such thing as getting away with it, in this life, past lives or future lives. It all eventually catches up with you.

Karma will continue until we all become spiritual masters. It begins and ends with love; unconditional love. If all you give out is love, all you receive will be love, the perfect life. We are all on a journey through the school of life until we master it. We are here to learn and gain wisdom. If you choose love, tolerance, forgiveness and compassion, the lessons will be easier to learn. Life will be a dream, problem-free and a pleasure to be a part of. The choice is yours.

We all get caught up in the karma of other people at some point in our lives, and we can worry and get involved, but this is the worst thing we can do. Instead, ask God to send them blessings, and ask the angels to help them sort themselves out. We can help other people but only if they ask for it. Giving it away is interfering, not the wisest thing to do, and can have repercussions.

Fortunately, we are moving into a new way of being, and soon Karma may be a thing of the past as we ascend to greater levels of consciousness. The more I have developed, the more clearly I can see that karma is merely a belief, a program in the matrix that creates consequences, albeit a deep-rooted one that is beyond our control.

11. Science and Karma

History contains many theories relating to science. Sir Isaac Newton was at the forefront of documented scientific facts and figures when he published his Laws of Motion in the 17th Century. At the time, his views were radical, and explained that the universe is a huge mechanical system, and that space and time are absolute within that system. Much later, towards the latter part of the 19th Century, new research suggested that other forces also existed that could not be explained by Newtonian physics. Collectively, these were referred to as Field Theory. Research by James Clerk Maxwell and Michael Faraday led to the discovery of fields of energy. They stated that these fields closely interacted with one another.

By 1900 Quantum Physics became part of the new world theories, when Max Planck put forward his theory of the world as a burst of 'Quanta.' This showed that matter consisted of a burst of various possibilities and probabilities, rather than being absolute, as Newton had believed. This developed into a whole new way of looking at things, and suggested that reality, as we perceive it, may not be so real or solid at all. This new thinking evolved into what we now know as Quantum Theory, based on relative physics. This was Albert Einstein's view of the Universe, contradicting Newton by stating that the universe was relative rather than absolute. This meant that it was always changing. He suggested that time and space were inseparable, co-existing as a fourth dimension.

Towards the end of the 20th Century, String Theory and M-Theory were proposed. These suggested that every single thing we can see in our reality, when broken down into its smallest particles, consists of strings of energy or light, all vibrating at different frequencies. This understanding helped to connect many of the previous scientific theories and in 1984 was formally accepted as the mainstream scientific view.

Maybe one day a single, unified theory will be discovered that unites all of the other theories relating to the holographic nature of our world and beyond. The reality we see with our human eyes and the realms we see with our mind's eye. The one thing we do know is that we live in a matrix;

we have created a holographic reality that reflects our beliefs, feelings and emotions.

What connects Science and Karma? Well, if every action prompts a reaction, it must be either a positive or a negative reaction. There cannot be no reaction at all, and therefore we are all creators. I was taught that we all have God within us (I use God as a general term of reference. I leave it open to your own understanding to use whatever term you feel comfortable with). I never really understood this, but if God is the Creator and we can create using thought, speech and by what we do, we must have the power of creation within us—the ability to manifest certain things in our lives. Not on the same level as the power of God, the creator of all that is, of course, but the power to create nevertheless. This being the case, we must create our own lives to some degree, if not completely.

I once worked with a man who was very unforgiving of other peoples' shortcomings, and bad mouthed them constantly for silly mistakes they had made booking in his clients. One night, he had all four of his tyres slashed; he moaned and groaned about it for days. What he did not realise was that he was only producing more negativity and the cycle continued. His clients would either cancel appointments or turn up late. This did not happen to the other therapists. They did not moan about things that went wrong, they were much more relaxed.

Maybe if he had been more tolerant and less volatile, producing more positive energy, the reaction might not have happened, or maybe he would have only had one tyre slashed instead. Most of us have had some form of negativity hit us at one point or another, due to our ignorance or innocence of how life works. Nobody is perfect!

From my experience, I believe that the best way to break the cycle is to treat the trying times as a test; we are all at the school of life after all. We are here to learn, whether we like it or not. If we choose to treat problems in life as a test, let's say we get a flat tyre for example; we can either fail by getting angry, which just produces more negativity to come back on us in the future, or we can take a deep breath and deal with it calmly and think *"Oh well, these things happen."* and learn the lesson. Do that and we have passed; it is easy when we know how. After all, we must have deserved the flat tyre, that's the way life works. The Universe sends it right back at us. So, just let it go, get it fixed, and concentrate on positive thoughts, words and actions. Simple!

There is meaning in everything, even a flat tyre. A flat tyre could be sent to slow you down; it could be the result of negative Karma or it could mean that you are feeling flat or deflated, either emotionally or physically. If it happens to you, just ask your higher self the question, *"What is this trying to tell me?"* And the first thing that comes into your mind is the answer.

When you act with Grace you create more positive energy for the future. Remember the saying, *'What goes around comes around'*? It really does! When you stop and think, you will start to realise all things happen for a reason. On the other hand, when you are kind, considerate and forgiving, most, if not all, of the energy that you produce is positive, which means a brighter future.

You will begin to notice the good things that happen to you along your journey. You may get the fantastic job you were looking for and the great salary, or you may find the bargain you have been looking for when you are shopping or a parking space just where you need it instead of miles away: these little things count too! Basically, you get what you deserve, good or bad.

Accept it and move on. If things are bad in your life change how you live, fix it. If you need help, ask for it, ask the Universe. If you don't ask, you don't get! You are creating your own life, remember. Moaning or over-analysing is time and energy wasted. It can send you around the bend. Enjoy the good things, give thanks, and treat every day like it is your first and last. Live for today, in the moment, that is all there is, this moment, right now. The past is gone, it no longer exists and the future has not happened yet, it does not exist, not in this dimension, anyway. There is only now!

If you find it hard to let go or relax, find some help. There are many ways available. For example, meditation or relaxation tapes or CDs are worth a try, perhaps a complementary or alterative therapy. The choices are vast but the advice is do not ignore your body's telltale signs. Find the cause of the problem and get some help. If you ignore it, it will only get worse and damage your health and future happiness.

Out of the many people I have met over the years, I have noticed that the ones who were happy, cheerful and laid back had better lives on all levels. They were successful, and the right kind of people came into their lives to help them on their journey. Like attracts like. Generally they were healthier and they were a pleasure to be around. Their light shone, so to speak. The ones that had a dream to fulfil and were positive and worked hard to get there, usually did. On the other hand, the people who were aggressive, complained a lot or treated other people badly were not much fun to be around at all; in fact I avoided them like the plague. They seemed to have a lot of what they called *"bad luck"*; things just did not seem to go their way. If only they could see that they were creating their own bad luck, they might have changed their ways. Karma was intervening once again. You cannot escape it!

I need to make clear here that I believe not everything that happens to you is a result of your actions in this life. Some events have been pre-determined and agreed to by you, prior to your incarnation (before you were born) for your own development; lessons you have not yet learned, and things you need to experience in order to grow as a person. The chapter about Karma explain this further. It is, of course, up to you whether you choose to believe this or not, but whilst it may appear mind-blowing, it does make a lot of sense.

The question is: Are we in a cycle of events in a matrix governed by mathematics and geometry, or are we on a spiritual journey to reach enlightenment, and all that we see around us is just an illusion in which to learn our lessons? A great big holographic school, if you like. Having looked into both of these options in depth, both make perfect sense; the connection is there—the scientific and spiritual theories that explain creation, and the meaning of life.

This book is intended to inspire you to find your own Divine Truth, not to make you believe what I believe. Please do your own research, on the internet, in books, go to talks, seminars and workshops to search for the answers, and if only one person who does that changes their life for the better, this book will have been worth writing.

There is more to consider regarding the connection between science and spirit. Mediums and clairvoyants connect this solid world with the spirit world. Whilst it is true that there are some charlatans out there, many are acting with integrity. Like it or not, or believe it or not, some of them are amazing. Having said that, if you do visit them, bear in mind that spirit has no concept of time as we see it, in days, months and years. The 24-hour clock is man-made, for us to keep track of where we are and to put order into our lives. Spirit sees the past, present and future all together. So if you are told that you will meet the man or woman of your dreams next Thursday, it may not be spot on.

Many spiritual mediums and clairvoyants only inform you of one path, only one possible outcome in your future which, of course, could change. It all depends on where you are in your life journey now, and what you want to happen in your future. As you know, as humans we change our minds continuously as to what we want, especially when we are young. What they tell you could change too.

For example if you suddenly change your job or move house, you may have turned a different corner, and thus changed your future. In changing your path you are now heading down a new one with new manifestations along the way. I am not saying that these people are wrong, I am just pointing out that not all you are told is carved in stone. You can change things either knowingly or unknowingly. Mediums and clairvoyants help a lot of people and are a strong connection between this dimension and other realms of existence, but check out their reputation first before you part with your money.

12. *The Bigger Picture*

We all have the Divine spark within us, and together we create the whole. What you see in this world at the moment, through the eyes of world media, is the result of a fear-based society, mixed up in a horrid cocktail of humanity's negative karma. We are being given the opportunity to repair this damage, to fix the broken souls we have become, and to evolve into a higher level of being, with pure intentions in our hearts and minds. I know it sounds too big a task but we have a lot of divine assistance, and it is not only possible but also necessary for us to change. It must happen; the Divine Plan will be carried out in accordance with God's will. It sounds more difficult than it really is, but we can do it. If we do a little something to help ourselves and pray for God's Will to be done, that alone will help tremendously.

There is a universal formula that states that the square root of 1% of the population will be enough to change the holographic world we live in, to create a shift in consciousness. That's not many when you think about it. In a world of approximately seven billion people, it is only about 8000. This is the minimum needed to start the ball rolling in the right direction, and change is already upon us. In July 2012, during one of my meditations, I was informed that we have already reached this figure, which is fantastic news. The sky is showing the colours of the rainbow, as more light enters the planet. Good things are happening, but the mainstream media generally only informs us of the bad stuff. However, more and more of us are waking up and doing our bit to help with the ascension process. Fear is the biggest problem, as it keeps mankind trapped in base mentality, causing the fight or flight mode to ignite, and from that perspective people tend to fight. By raising awareness and releasing fear, we can raise our vibration and respond from a higher level of consciousness. It is the wise choice really, the changes are happening now, and we are all a part of the Divine Plan.

Science tells us that we live in a matrix, a holographic reality that reflects our beliefs, feelings and emotions; our desires, goals and fears are played out for us to learn lessons in order that we can grow. The world acts as a mirror to our consciousness; we are constantly being shown our loves and our deepest fears.

The three basic patterns of fear are related to abandonment and separation, low self-worth, and fear of surrender and trust. These fear-based thoughts, desires and beliefs create the negative aspects of not only our daily lives but the reality of the whole planet. This mass of fear-based creative energy is the main problem. The only way to rectify the hologram is to remove the fear through self-healing, prayer and education based on spiritual growth, and to replace that fear with love and compassion. We need to connect to our higher minds and our divinity once more. Maybe you should look up the word lightworker, and see if you feel a calling to help in some way. Some lightworkers are teachers, others are therapists and practitioners, some just need to look after their own families and be the best examples they can.

Whatever choice we make, what is important is that we wake up and take back our power. That way we control the hologram, and not give our power away to governments and religious leaders to control mass consciousness through feeding us fear via the media.

If we want peace, we must be peaceful
If we want trust, we must trust one another
If we want love, we must love ourselves and one another
If we want compassion, we must forgive one another.

Our world is the creation of our messed-up thoughts, feelings and emotions being reflected in a God-given hologram based on Karmic consequences. What goes around comes around, to use an old aphorism. You only get out what you put in. Anger creates more anger, and fear creates more fearful experiences. We act out all of these situations until we figure it out and change into better people. We need to work through our negative karma and evolve into purer beings of light in this beautiful mystery school called Earth. That is why the planet was created and why we are here, to incarnate into physical bodies, in order to learn about sexuality, emotional expression and feelings through experiencing them all.

Many people believe that we are Spirit inhabiting a body that acts as a temporary chariot for our life on this planet, where free will reigns supreme in order to help us to develop. One big experiment that began way back in Lemuria and Atlantis, designed to help us raise our frequency in order to become enlightened beings once more. That is why there is a need for the complementary and alternative therapies and medicines. Many people are remembering old skills and using herbs, crystals, sound, colour and other healing aids to repair the damage, and re-awaken our original 12-strand DNA blueprint, to enable us to re-connect with Source and live in peace once more, as the pure souls we once were.

It is said that we are all ascending and so are the planets and indeed the whole of creation. This does not mean we are all going to float up into heaven. It is about bringing the divine energies down into the planet, bringing heaven to earth, by raising our own vibration and that of our planet too. Many people have raised their consciousness to higher levels; this refers to the mind. But we also need to raise the vibration of the body by purifying it, and in turn activating our higher levels of DNA. It is the high vibration bodies that will act as anchors for the new Earth energies.

Every living thing on this planet is here to evolve; plants are here to develop mind; animals to develop feelings; and man to develop unconditional love and compassion, to become enlightened by finding the path back to Source and Oneness, as it was in Atlantis. Once these new energies are anchored into the planet, we will be living in a new world, free from the confines of the old controlling ways. Individual spirituality will be the way forward; a one-to-one relationship with God will be formed. The man-made aspects of religion, based on fear and control, will be gone forever. Amen to that.

In Atlantis it is believed that we were very highly evolved, spiritually enlightened souls, with amazing healing and telepathic abilities, but it did not leave much scope for growth, and evolution was slow because of this. Atlantis fell from grace when a group of high priests became greedy for power. This led to segregation, fear took form, and Atlantis, as an experiment, was terminated by the great floods.

The few who were saved carried divine knowledge within their blueprints. The experiment began again, only this time karma was introduced and we have been in a world, created by us, in a state of cause and effect ever since.

The more mankind became greedy for power, the more fearful people became, and as a result, certain chakras were closed down in order for them to survive. This meant that people were vibrating at a much lower frequency. Mankind drifted further from the God Source, and less light prevailed as a result. Eventually most people forgot that they were divine sparks of God altogether, and the healing and telepathic abilities disappeared as the chakras were closed down. The original high frequency DNA functions were shut down, causing the related information and healing capabilities to diminish, as a result of becoming more distant from the Divine. It is time to reawaken those skills and THE TIME IS NOW!

13. Dimensions—Physical and Non-Physical

In general, most of us believe that the solid world we see with our eyes, the physical world of time and space, consists of separate elements. This could not be further from the truth. For a start, time and space are not separate entities; they only appear to be that way because of our perception of reality. We look at creation through 3D eyes and see only solid matter, and we call it the physical world; solid and separate. We may also believe it to be unaffected by the past and future, but this is not true either.

It is obvious that life has been affected by the past, but influences from the future are not so obvious. In the non-physical world there is no time and space; the past, present and the future all exist at the same time; they are all happening at the same time. Therefore the present is affected by the past and the future because they co-exist in the non-physical realms of creation, and a change in one immediately affects all.

On that basis, since all things are interrelated, everything has a level of consciousness and memory. In the non-physical world of dimensions, all things are truly connected to one another and therefore to the whole, hence Oneness! This being the case, things do not just exist in one dimension at any one time. They exist in other levels of reality, in other dimensions, and any one act can have a small or large effect on another level, which is removed in time and space, thus creating change in both the physical and non-physical realms. Our simple laws of physics cannot always explain these events and the effects they may have in our physical world. This means that there is a lot more to us, the world we live in, the Universe and the whole of creation than we have previously perceived.

We are, in general, inexperienced in the working and understanding of these 'other worlds' or realms of existence and 'spiritual dimensions'. Because of their immediate effect on our 3D world, maybe now it is time for us to learn more, to communicate and to evolve accordingly into the multidimensional beings of light we truly are. It is time to break down the barriers and join with our brothers and sisters from these other realms.

First, we need to forget about the more conventional laws of physics, and edge more towards the laws of quantum physics by looking at the principles of 'probability' and 'uncertainty'. Quantum mechanics is a theory of many parallel Universes. The difference between one Universe and the next can be so small, maybe only one photon, but the reality in that world could be vastly different from ours—it takes all sorts to make a Super Universe!

Reality does not consist of only one dimension but, in general, we can only see one of them, namely the 3rd dimension. This is, or course, unless you are clairvoyant or you know how to journey through meditation. Then the possibilities are endless.

In the chapter on Meditation later in this book I refer to crystal skulls. I believe that the crystal skulls will help mankind to evolve into higher levels of consciousness and perception; connected on a higher level and capable of inter-dimensional travel, if only through meditation techniques. The Merkaba is our light body, which is said to help us travel to other dimensions through meditation. Maybe our Merkaba will take us where we need to go? Think of it as a kind of flying saucer made of light, capable of taking us through portals when we are meditating, and enabling us to explore the matrix of consciousness. This is pretty mind-blowing stuff but nevertheless it is easier than one would think. If travelling to other dimensions sounds weird, consider this: 500 years ago we thought that the world was flat! Try not to work this out with a 'rational' mind; you are a light being with amazing super-human abilities—you just need to open your mind and believe.

Many people assume that science proves metaphysics to be false; that all things relating to God, heaven, hell and the soul, for example, do not exist. This is the view of sceptics, not scientists. In this age of quantum physics, these invisible entities and energies may be shown to exist in other realms and in parallel dimensions. We live in a kind of psychic soup. Just because you cannot see these other beings does not mean that they are not there.

There appear to be many different dimensions and I have listed the main ones I am aware of below. Many of these are referred to in The Urantia Book, an amazing encyclopaedia of information relating to the whole of creation. This was first published by the Urantia foundation in 1955.

LOCAL UNIVERSE
1st Dimension - Mineral Kingdom
2nd Dimension - Plant Kingdom
3rd Dimension - Humans and Animals
4th Dimension - Astral and Interplanetary Souls
5th Dimension - Extraterrestrial Beings
6th Dimension - Ultra terrestrial Beings

Similar to an Extraterrestrial, the so-called "Ultra terrestrials" are creatures that come from other dimensions, as opposed to other planets.

SUPERUNIVERSE
7th Dimension - Ascended Masters (Parent race to 4D)
8th Dimension - Galactic Masters (Parent race to 5D)
9th Dimension - Multi-Dimensional Over souls (Parent race to 6D)

CENTRAL UNIVERSE
10th Dimension - Timeline Engineers
11th Dimension - Time Lords
12th Dimension - Founders of Universes
13th Dimension - Central Universe Administration
14th Dimension - Central Universe Headquarters
15th Dimension - Paradise Trinity

It would appear from this list that there is quite a lot going on out there!

14. Angels and Ascended Masters

We are very fortunate to have amazing light beings in this dimension, helping us through the changes on the planet, as we move through the evolutionary change to higher levels of consciousness. These beings are by our side day and night, helping us and guiding us. Recently, I sensed that the unicorn energy had arrived. These beautiful beings of light leave a feather as a calling card, just like the Angels. They are full of light and are more than willing to help us to become enlightened. But we need to ask for help and guidance, as light beings can only intervene in free will where there is a life-threatening situation. If we do not ask for their help, they cannot help us.

Angels can help with the simplest of things, from finding a parking space to helping you put together a dinner party. They love to help and you can show your appreciation by playing them beautiful music and singing for them. I do this often, and it makes me feel very emotional and connected to my divine helpers.

We can also ask the Ascended Masters to help us. My favourites are Archangel Michael, Archangel Gabriel, Archangel Uriel and Archangel Raphael. Whenever I am working, I call upon these mighty Archangels and ask them to stand at the four points, north, south, east and west, to guide and protect me as I work. Archangel Michael, in my eyes, is the heart and soul of Crystal Ki Healing. He helps with the tie cutting, which is essential to clearing negative energies, entities and ETs, and releasing us from negative attachments.

It is possible to write to some of the Ascended Masters, the Karmic Board, as it were, twice a year for dispensation and sponsorship. The Karmic Board is an eight member board of Ascended Masters who dispense justice to the souls on this planet. They consist of the following:

- The Great Divine Director
- The Goddess of Liberty
- Lady Master Nada
- Elohim Cyclopea

- Pallas Athena, twin flame of the Maha Chohan
- Lady Master Portia, St Germain's twin flame
- Quan Yin, Goddess of Mercy
- The Dhyani Buddha Vairochana

We all know these Masters as we have passed before them many times before, and after every incarnation on this planet. They are there to adjudicate Karma, mercy and judgement. These Masters have complete, unrestricted access to our Akashic records. These records contain all information about us, and the whole of creation. It is a kind of etheric library, which we can access through meditation.

We can write to them twice a year to give gratitude, seek divine guidance asking for resolutions to our earthly problems, and for dispensation. We can also ask for help and sponsorship with our earthly missions. This mighty board meet on New Years Eve and on the 4th July at the Royal Teton Retreat. This is when the petitions are read and dispensations awarded as deserved.

Every six months we are given the opportunity to look at our lives, make offerings to God, surrender our bad habits, etc. It is best to under-promise and over-deliver in our petitions. We can do this by writing a letter to the Karmic board as follows:

The letter must be hand written during the fourteen days before the meeting at the Retreat. Include your offering to God, what you are willing to resolve in your shortcomings, and what you are requesting dispensation or sponsorship with. Keep a copy of the letter and consecrate (meaning to set aside with divine intent) the original by creating a small alter or sacred space. On the said date, ask your Guardian Angel to take the letter to the Karmic Board on your behalf. They will take the information, not the physical letter; you need to burn the letter after you have requested your Angel to take it to the Retreat. Then it is a matter of having faith and seeing what happens next. You can meditate and ask to be taken to speak to Lady Master Nada or any other member of the Board you feel drawn to, and ask if your requests are to be granted.

15. New Energies and Transitional Problems

This planet is being flooded with new solar, cosmic and galactic energies. Even the magnetic grid around the planet is altering to suit the new Earth frequencies. We are all being upgraded to a higher frequency, and many can feel each shift as it happens. Energy is constantly changing and we must go with the flow and incorporate these new energies into our energy fields as we evolve with Mother Earth into higher levels of consciousness, otherwise referred to as ascension, or the ascension process.

Many people can feel the process taking place, though some are suffering as a consequence, with illness and tiredness being the main problems. We also become less tolerant of harmful, negative environments than we once were.

These are, however, transitional problems, as we are becoming purer higher light beings and changing at a cellular level. As our consciousness rises, it can bring emotional and physical discomfort as we anchor our soul into our physical selves. Our internal organs become less dense as they no longer hold and express the emotions that they used to. As the cells change and become less dense, the human body systems have more work to do processing these changes, and we become tired as a result.

As aches and pains come and go, doctors often have difficulty explaining these problems. People can have palpitations as the heart chakra realigns itself to the higher energies. Psychic abilities increase as we awaken dormant DNA, previously considered to be junk DNA. There is also a slight increase in the brain size, which can cause headaches. Not everyone suffers these transitional conditions, and the best action is to rest, eat highly nutritious foods, and drink sufficient pure water. If we resist change, the soul will allow us to become ill until we work through our issues and release them completely.

It is common to see the numbers 11:11 in ratio form when going through transition (moving from one level of consciousness to the next), and this is a signpost that we need to take extra care with eating properly, getting adequate rest and retreating, if necessary. I always feel wide open when I am between levels, and the transition is heartfelt. I can feel very emotional as I release old energies and belief systems, but once they have been released

I feel invigorated. I state clearly to the Universe that I accept this new level of consciousness. It is important to make this statement in order to fully anchor your new level of consciousness and the energy it brings with it. Having not bothered to state this in the past, I noticed that I stayed in transition much longer than necessary, which meant I felt vulnerable and lost as if I was neither here nor there. Now I do this to anchor myself mentally into this new level of consciousness.

When I am in transition I feel far more sensitive to all energies that are around me, and the best thing I find to do at these times is to stay at home and keep clearing out old energies, working through what needs to be released.

As we reach higher levels of consciousness and change at a cellular level, we become closer to Source and therefore more powerful co-creators. As we continue to raise our vibration, it is important to realise that we have more power, and to use that power wisely. Not being ready for the higher levels would be like giving the keys of a Ferrari to a learner driver; a disaster in the making. In order to reach the top, we must accept this new responsibility, and hence a new way of life.

When I first woke up to the changes taking place on the planet and to healing, my Angels became my new best friends, in particular Archangel Michael, and he has always been around me and protects me when I need him. We are on first name terms and he was the first contact I had with these Divine Beings. My Guardian Angel has been a great help to me over the years as well, and I am truly grateful.

The main Archangels are the representatives of the seven rays of life and they retreat at certain, special places on the planet. Ascended Masters were once in human form and gained mastery over the material planes; they balanced at least 51% of their negative karma and fulfilled their Divine Plan; they are God-like and united in their own presence (God-self). By simply saying out loud, or in your mind, the following words, you can call upon these Wise Beings for help:

Affirm … *I call upon the Ascended Masters to help and guide me today.*

If you know, work with, or are familiar with the name of a particular Master or Archangel, just insert their name instead. Say the affirmation three times and they will come, they always do. All of these beings are here with us. You do not have to be 'special' to connect with them; just have an open mind and an open heart.

16. Atlantis, DNA and Indigo Children

It is recorded that in Atlantis many different types of spiritual beings from different corners of the universe incarnated into a human template. There was no illness, no sadness, everybody was pure, and therefore there was no karma. People traded with one another and there was plenty for everybody. This was before the fall from grace. It only took a few of the high priests to make some wrong choices, and the beautiful perfection was ruined.

At the time, we were all healers, we were all telepathic. We were capable of inter-dimensional travel; we had super human strengths and abilities. Apparently we also had many more strands of DNA fully functioning, as opposed to the two strands of DNA we were subsequently reduced to. These priests interfered with the brain, splitting it into the two sections of logic and intuition, in order to stop our telepathy. They did not want us to know what they were thinking.

After a while, telepathic powers ceased to work correctly, and this is when verbal language evolved and people became divided into groups. This once perfect place was now contaminated with fear and other negative emotions; we began to lose the ability to use these strands of DNA to their full capacity. Atlantis became so contaminated that it had to be destroyed.

Most of the people on this planet are said to originate from other worlds, other planets. This may sound crazy, but nevertheless I believe it to be true. Many of us have stellar origins as either star people or Angels, and have been born at this time for a reason. That reason is to help with the current changes and the Ascension process. We are in the process of reactivating our original strands of DNA. The strands that were disconnected, were unravelled and implants were put in to stop them reconnecting.

The repercussions had a detrimental effect on the pineal gland, the pituitary gland and the hypothalamus gland, and these glands have shrunken in size through lack of use.

Implants can be removed by competent healers, and our original blueprint can be re-activated through healing meditation and prayer. We are gradually reconnecting and rebuilding DNA. When the numbers 11:11 are brought to your attention, your DNA is upgrading. The 11:11 is a signal or code that triggers changes in your DNA. These changes have been happening for years and none of us now have only the original two strands; we have all been upgraded to connect with higher levels.

There have been children born throughout the last century that have more than two active strands of DNA, to help raise the vibration of the planet. They are very intelligent, loving and amazingly gifted children; they shine with a vibrant energy.

17. Autistic Spectrum Disorders

There are various ways of looking at Autistic Spectrum Disorders (ASD), Attention Deficit Hyperactivity Disorder (ADHD), Attention Deficit Disorder (ADD) and Aspergers Syndrome.

Many people dwell on the negative aspects of these and often only see poor social skills, obsessive behaviours and hyperactivity problems. This has led to labelling children and adults with the 'special needs' badge, which really annoys them and can lead to internalised anger and rage. Many people would not be able to differentiate between these two separate emotions. Most of us understand rage to mean just a more extreme form of anger. However rage could be described as powerless anger. By powerless I mean having no control over what is happening to you, or that you have no means of expressing your feelings. Internalised rage can be a major health problem on all levels—in some cases a volcano waiting to erupt. This is a particularly prevalent within people who have been victims of abuse. People who are labelled as 'different' with a negative connotation are often suffering with rage. Rage needs to be healed as a separate emotion.

I recently read a brilliant book called 'Healing ADD: the breakthrough program that allows you to see and heal the 6 types of ADD' by Daniel G. Amen, M.D. Using brain imaging, SPECT studies, this neuroscientist and psychiatrist has evidence of the disorder being a physical brain function problem wherein the prefrontal cortex, or another area of the brain, does not function correctly or even at all, when the person is trying to do tasks that require concentration. This leads to problems in school, not because of low intelligence but because the brain is not working correctly.

Drugs like Ritalin, Dexetrine and Adderall are often used, even by Dr Amen, to help symptoms but he also uses other natural remedies, including supplements like St John's Wart, L-tyrosine and DL-phenylalanine, a high protein, low carbohydrate diet (eliminating sugar, bread, potatoes, pasta and rice), and intense aerobic exercise. I highly recommend reading this book if you have a child with ADD, ADHD or even OCD and the like.

Note: Blood type 'O' people should never use St John's Wart. Always contact your doctor and herbalist before taking St John's Wart as there is a long list of contraindications associated with this herb.

In my experience many of these children are talented individuals but not necessarily due to their condition. Some appear to have incarnated at a higher frequency and are therefore more spiritually evolved. Others appear to be much more evolved and can, for example, be clairvoyant, clairsentient, or clairaudient. They can also be telepathic, with immense psychic powers and natural healing abilities. Some of these children can turn lights on and off without touching them, and recharge batteries with their minds. According to age they are referred to as Indigo children, Crystal children or Rainbow children, depending on when they were born and the colours in their energy field.

Indigo children tend to have the warrior spirit and will clear the way for the more delicate and sensitive Crystal children. The Rainbow children are highly evolved souls, and actually look like angels with an amazing amount of light around them. Their wisdom can be profound, as if they have lived many previous lives, and some can clearly remember these.

It is important to speak to these children in an appropriate manner, as they do not understand abstract concepts or ambiguous language like slang. I once had a teacher tell me that a child was being rude, as when he was told that he needed to pull his socks up, meaning to work a bit harder, he looked down at them and replied, *"They ARE up"*. Autistic children take things very literally and this can be distressing, it is important to teach them what certain sayings mean.

These children also do not respond well to commands, and it is important to give them a choice, by asking them to do something rather than telling them. Telling someone to carry out a task is interfering with free will and is not spiritually correct behaviour; these children are very wise and spiritually evolved and need to be treated accordingly.

If you have a child in this category, the best thing I can advise you to do is to get them grounded, take them to a crystal shop, and let them choose the crystals they need as their intuition will guide them to the correct ones for them. Read about Crystal, Indigo and Rainbow children and find out more about their abilities, and focus on the positive aspects before you, or others, do them harm by labelling them as mentally disabled.

18. *The Conscious and the Sub-Conscious Mind*

In order to break and release old habits, negative belief patterns and behaviours and so on, we need to clear the programming from the sub-conscious mind. The sub-conscious part of the mind has six main functions:

- to act as a memory bank
- to form the seat of our imagination and of our emotions
- to regulate our heartbeat and breathing
- to hold onto patterns and beliefs
- it is responsible for the drive and motivation of the energy we have.
- to respond to repetition. This can be altered by using affirmations, one of my favourites being *"I am healthy, wealthy and wise,"* which seems to cover everything.

The logical mind is responsible for reasoning and logical behaviour. You use your logical mind to move your hand to pick up a book or to choose a place you want to go and eat, or to add and subtract for example. By consciously repeating an affirmation we can train the sub-conscious mind to accept the affirmation as a belief.

Things can go wrong for us when we are repeatedly told, for example, that we are stupid or that we are not good enough, or that we are fat or ugly. This can programme our sub-conscious mind into believing these comments and they become parts of us, stored in our memory banks. They can lead to all kinds of mental and emotional hang-ups, which can eventually filter through to manifest as an actual physical illness, perhaps even cancer.

In a positive light, we can train the sub-conscious mind to act as an auto-pilot for us. Take learning to ride a bike. At first it is difficult and we must learn to concentrate on more than one thing at once and all working in unison, peddling, steering, and direction. However, after a short while, with some repetition and practice, we can jump on the bike and ride it steadily, without even having to think about it, with the sub-conscious doing most of the work for us. The same goes for driving a car, we do not have to think every time we change gear or turn the steering wheel, it just comes naturally via the sub-conscious programming, as a result of practise.

It is possible to reprogram negative beliefs and behaviour, and it usually takes around 21 days to programme the mind. And re-programming using clearing techniques also takes 21 days.

The sub-conscious mind is in control of our emotions, such as fear and anxiety, and all automatic emotional responses. Fear and anxiety are forms of energy, and can therefore be removed by tie-cutting and space-clearing (see chapter on Tie Cutting). This means that using the techniques in this book it is possible to remove fear and anxiety in one or two sessions. I have had fantastic results with anxious clients by removing their fear and anxiety.

Try to see your mind as a computer; your automatic emotional responses are programmes, as are all of your belief systems. For example, if you repeatedly saw your father get angry and violent when you were younger, your programming could respond in the same way to stressful situations, or make you so frightened that you just run away altogether. Either way, that is not the correct response to anger.

Anger needs to be released from the system as it may damage the liver if it is repressed; therefore the best thing to do is release the anger in a controlled manner. So if you need to lash out, punch the pillow, go for a brisk walk or count to ten and breathe out the anger.

By feeding your sub-conscious mind with the correct programming you can release old habits and belief systems and fix many personality problems. The conscious and sub-conscious minds form a team, and when programmed and working together correctly, they are absolutely brilliant, resulting in our emotions and our views on life being grounded and stable.

I used tie cutting to help me to reprogram my belief that I needed cigarettes. I would visualise the cigarette about five metres away from me and cut ties with it, stating this sentence—*"I cut and release you with love and peace, I am totally free"*. It is important to say this sentence as it releases the energy as well. Whenever I felt like a cigarette I would cut ties with it until I no longer wanted one. I did manage to kick the habit.

I did the same to release my belief that romantic love was a trap, although this time I visualised a disc of Crystal Ki light moving through my body and a net of light taking that belief system away. In my mind's eye I could actually see a heart and a cage being lifted away in the net. The chapter on Tie Cutting and Space Clearing explains this technique and how to perform it in more detail.

19. *The Mass Consciousness creates our World*

The collective consciousness of our thoughts and feelings creates the world we live in. We are the world; we are God, every living thing in existence is part of God. The thing that takes us away from that level of consciousness is fear. When fear is allowed to control our thoughts and feelings it runs wild creating the negative aspects of the violent world we can all see today.

We are responsible; through ignorance we have created this mess. The good news is we can repair it, not by battling to change the old one but by creating a new one and forcing the old to become obsolete. The only way to achieve this is to release the fear and replace it with peace. Peaceful hearts and minds create a peaceful world. It is not politicians and religious leaders who will create peace, it is us! En masse, we are the creative consciousness and therefore the Power. This is all to do with our light frequency or vibration and the holographic make up of the reality we live in.

Television, the internet, and the media pump us full of negative information and news, keeping us in a state of fear. When we are fearful, we are weak and a low frequency or vibration. Our God-given creative powers are therefore manipulated as a result of negative input.

The higher your frequency the more powerful a creator you become. We all have the divine spark within, and we all have the ability to create our lives, and to live in a beautiful, peaceful world. Broadcasting and printing bad news keeps the base chakra in a fight or flight mode of thought, thus keeping the whole planet trapped in a negative state of existence. Paedophilia, corruption and so-called terrorists groups are beamed to families as they sit in front of the television having dinner in the evening. This information can really be soul destroying. Your soul is pure and deserves pure input so why feed it this rubbish?

If you must watch television, try watching pre-recorded films and DVDs, to create the choice of watching something less damaging than live television. Try avoiding the news, television and newspapers for a week, if not for good, and see how much better you feel. I know some people may struggle with that as watching bad news can be addictive, but tuning in to watch a news program can fill your living space with fear and disharmony.

Instead, watch films that don't include violence, sex, or any subject that makes you feel sad, or otherwise disturbs you. Try listening to beautiful music, or even silence, all of which are healthier. The choice is yours.

I have some very bright friends who insist on reading newspapers, think these are essential to modern life, and believe that they are not being fooled because they can read between the lines, so to speak. However, the people who write the papers, write between the lines too, in order to influence the minds of intelligent people as well. Wake up! They have still had your attention on the subject of war or famine, for example, and your thoughts have been adding to the mass negativity as you read it, even whilst you thought you were reading between the lines. During the time you were reading about negative incidences you have been a low frequency creator amidst the mass consciousness.

It is difficult to read doom and gloom and send out positive energy at the same time, unless you know how to transmute your energy as you create it, and only an enlightened few know how to do that. This being the case, even the jolly, happy souls who read between the lines have to take responsibility for the state of the world. In fact, we all need to act and create the world we intend our children and grandchildren to live in, and then take action to make it happen.

Pharmaceutical companies make a fortune out of our illnesses and dis-ease. They lobby hard against complementary medicine, because when people consult natural health care practitioners, these companies lose money.

Research has shown that, during the Second World War, fluoride was used to keep populations in occupied countries and prisoners in prison camps docile, as fluoride suppressed the will centres in the mind. Even today, many countries add fluoride to their water supply. You may ask why they do that? I am also led to believe that fluoride can cause calcification of the pineal gland. This gland is the vital gateway that enables us to access other realms of existence through meditation and astral travel.

Food contains many additives, preservatives and colourings, which contaminate our systems. In many places in the world, cattle are given bovine growth hormones from a very young age, and when we consume this meat we ingest those hormones. According to Professor Jane Plant, these can cause problems such as breast and prostate cancer. She carried out extensive research into this, and cured her own breast cancer by altering her diet. Other chemicals found in cleaning products lower our frequency, as well as poisoning us and keeping us sick and reliant on the pharmaceutical companies. They make money; we stay sick and die! It is up to all of us to take control of our lives and do something about it. It is time to stop being lambs to the slaughter and act now. I recommend you investigate the dangers of the chemicals in your food and household environment, and realise that you could be poisoning yourself and your children.

By simply eating better you could prolong an active life. Ideally, organic food if possible, nothing processed or frozen, pre-packed foods, avoiding additives and preservatives. We owe it to ourselves and to our children to eat the best food we can.

Maybe take some exercise, as even a brisk walk for twenty minutes a day will help. By doing these things and drinking pure water (6 to 8 glasses per day) you will feel a lot better and raise your vibration.

Try to take a few deep breaths regularly and let the life force flow into your heart and mind. Rather than sitting in front of the television to have dinner, turn the TV off, sit around a table and talk with the family. Maybe go for a walk afterwards.

Try letting go of fear too, as it attracts fearful situations to you. Try to change the way you think and be more positive. If we all do this, it will enable us to take back control of our collective consciousness, and let our purer minds help to build a perfect world.

We can live without chemical drugs if we choose to eat well, be happy, exercise and live a balanced lifestyle. We are all beings of light with amazing self-healing abilities as part of our creative make-up. We have the power—but we must be pro-active, if only in a small way. It all helps; we are all ONE.

All we need to do is bring more light into the planet. This will show us the Divine Truth. Ask God to flush out the corruption, to bless and purify the politicians and the planet in general, allowing us to create a purer way of life—the life we would like for ourselves and for our children.

The Universe's energies are here to help but we need to ask for that help and we all need to do our bit. We can change the balance of light and dark on our planet with a little input each from a lot of people. Taking more care of our health and well-being is all we need to do.

It is important to know that the people who appear to be in control of our creative energy are living in fear themselves, even though they probably do not even realise it. People who crave money have fear of lack, people who crave power are fearful of losing control. Allocating blame is not the answer here, we need to educate and enlighten ourselves in order to move forward, to forgive not fight.

Take Ghandi for example; In my view, Ghandi was more powerful than the British Empire because of his light and spiritual level of consciousness; he was closer to God and hence more powerful than the Empire as a result. When we move closer to that Divine Source of love we raise not only our own vibration, but also the vibration of the whole planet, and help to make a better life for all concerned. The more light we bring into our world the brighter it will shine on the darkness. The corrupt will be moved peacefully out with light and compassion, not aggression and control. It is important to be pro-peace not anti-war; being anti-war means you are giving your energy to war, and not to peace.

If we are aggressive, we only add more darkness and keep things as they are. If you see corrupt officials as lost children, just as God would, it would be easier to let go of their shortcomings and instead to apply compassion, wisdom and peace. Try not to see them as sinners, but as having obstacles blocking them from that Divine Source. When we ask God to help those who are doing wrong, he immediately sends them higher frequency energy, which will help them to get closer to him. We have no right to judge. Only God has that right and he chooses forgiveness first, every time. Forgiveness is essential to the evolution of the planet.

We are all souls on our own journey through this mystery school and we are all at different levels. Everything is happening for a reason and within divine time limits. The corrupt exist because of fear-based thought forms and their lesson is to recognise and correct that. Whilst it is not for us to judge, we can take back our control and our energy, our power to create, and use it in more positive ways, thereby diminishing the shadows holding the world in this low frequency reality.

We now have the opportunity to raise our vibration, thus raising the vibration of the whole planet and all life on it. There is a Divine Plan at work and it will be carried out in accordance with Divine Will because the Universe cannot let mankind destroy this planet, as it would have a knock-on effect for all of creation, not just our galaxy. Mother Earth is on the path to ascension and so are we, whether we like it or not. Some don't like it, but I say, *"Bring it on!"*

The Angels, star people and other beings of light are here to help us and guide us along the way. If you find it hard to believe in and accept these divine helpers, try to understand the science of creation through which you are creating this world and your future now, with everything you say, do, think and feel. So why not start thinking purer thoughts and create a beautiful world, free from fear-based behaviour. You do not need to be specific. Your ego self is not wise enough to choose a perfect world—your perfect world might be full of super models or pink fluffy bunnies, perfect for you maybe, but maybe not for the rest of us.

You need only think of a world that is full of unconditional love, trust, peace and compassion. *"May God's will be done. Amen."* Saying this statement alone helps to do the trick. You may like to say it when you wake in the morning and again when you go to bed at night. If more of us just said this simple sentence regularly, it could have a huge impact in bringing heaven down to earth. A little prayer goes a long way when said by a lot of people.

Learning to connect to your higher self and to meditate can help. It does not mean you need to sit in the lotus position like some kind of Buddha for hours on end. You can connect to your higher self by simply visualising a line of light, acting as a communication cable, descending from a gold sphere, representing your higher self, about 12 inches (30cm) above the top of your head. Then imagine it floating down into your head, down the front of your spine and into your heart centre. You will then be connected to your higher self and if you do this first thing in the morning, you can ask your higher self to guide your thoughts, words and deeds. If this is done regularly it won't be long before you notice your behaviour and thought processes improving.

If you set the intention to connect to your higher self, you will be connected. Your higher self will always guide you. All you need to do is to ask the question and wait for the answers. If you hear a voice that gives you a message to do something bad, then there is a good chance you have a negative spirit attached to you. My advice would be to ignore it and demand it leaves you alone. If it does not leave, you can carry out a tie-cutting as explained later in this book, or you may need to find a spiritual healer who can move it on for you.

You can meditate while sitting in the comfort of your own home or walking in the park. It is easy and anyone can do it, and what is more, it's free. You could be cooking a meal or painting your home. It does not matter, as long as you feel lost in the moment and relaxed, and the usual mind chatter is ignored or has ceased during your meditative session. It is all food for the soul.

20. The Map of Consciousness

Dr David Hawkins created what he called The Map of Consciousness. This enables us to calibrate where we are on the spiritual path in relation to consciousness, the journey back to source, and total self-realisation.

As we move forward and release old issues and learn more about spirituality and ascension, we progress through various areas in the Map of Consciousness, such as love and wisdom. The emotions we feel and the processes we go through during those changes are listed, and the God view and life view we feel, as a result of certain levels of attainment.

The lowest level in the map is Shame followed by Guilt, Apathy, Fear, Anxiety, Anger, and then Pride. All of these states of consciousness make the person feel weak. They are all low frequency levels, calibrated on the map as below the number 200. Once we transcend these levels there is a breakthrough, considered the level of integrity and courage. People at 200 or above on the scale become much stronger and have more spiritual power.

Sir Albert Einstein and Sir Isaac Newton were at 499, and they were stuck at the level of intellect, just below the second major transition point on the scale at 500—the level of real love.

The music of Louis Armstrong calibrates at 590; the book *A Course in Miracles Work Book*, tested at 600; this book calibrates at 740. Ghandi was at 760.

The higher the level, the closer to God and to self-realisation we become. Life becomes easier as we release our emotions and keep moving towards pure consciousness. As you reach the 600 level you radiate peace, the level of unconditional love. According to Dr Hawkins, approximately 50% of people who reach this 600 level leave the planet, and do so of their own free will. The rest choose to stay behind and help with the ascension process. Jesus, Buddha and Krishna calibrated at 1000. Apparently, this was the highest level the human nervous system could cope with in these earlier times, but things do change and the energetic nervous system and DNA are upgraded as we progress in order to channel the higher vibrations.

Even since writing the first edition of this book, the calibration levels have greatly increased throughout humanity and I have channelled a new Crystal Ki Map of Consciousness in my third book, 'The Princess & the Pink Moon Leeches. The new map goes up to 11,000 Time Lord Level and currently many of my students are calibrating at very high levels, having used the Crystal Ki techniques.

This original map is fully explained in the book called *'Power vs. Force'* by Dr David Hawkins. His audio programme entitled *'The Highest Level of Enlightenment'* is also very interesting. Even if your conscious mind cannot understand all of the information, your soul will understand every word, thus raising your vibration by just listening to it.

Dr Hawkins and his colleagues created the Map of Consciousness using Kinesiology Testing, or K-testing as it is sometimes called.

Kinesiology Testing

It is necessary to do these tests with another person. Before you start, it is important to remove all watches and jewellery, and to remain detached from the outcome. It is also important that both of you calibrate above 200 on the Map of Consciousness, which is the level of integrity, to get good clear results.

Now, the two of you should face one another a few feet apart. The tester places their right hand on the shoulder of the person being tested. The tested person puts out their right arm to the side, parallel to the ground, and at 90 degrees to the body. They close their eyes while the tester presses down two fingers on the outstretched wrist of the test subject whilst saying *"Resist"*. The test subject should be able to resist the pressure easily as the tester repeats this.

Next, the subject is asked to think of something they love and something that makes them happy. The tester then applies the same two finger downward pressure on the wrist exercise, and the subject should be able to resist easily.

The subject is then asked to think of something that makes them unhappy or sad, and the same process of two fingers pressing down on the wrist is applied. This time, however, the test subject is unable to resist and the arm will go weak and move downwards.

Another K-test to try is for the test subject to hold something to be tested in their left hand holding it to their solar plexus, just below their heart and in the centre of their ribcage. For example, use an apple. To test if apples are good for the subject, apply pressure to the subject's wrist just as before. If apples are good for the subject, the arm will not move down. It is important to give declarations rather than ask questions.

By doing these tests both the tester and the test subject should get good ideas as to what gives a good, strong positive response, or a weak or non-response. The principle about this test is that truth and integrity have an anabolic, positive effect on your field of consciousness, whilst false, non-integrous things will have a catabolic, negative impact on the field. You can use this to test foods, flower remedies, music, or colours, for example, or whatever you like.

The results may be affected if, for example, negative emotions, such as grief are blocking the energy centres of the test subject. These can be temporarily removed by using the thymus thump. The thymus gland is located behind the sternum just beneath the clavicle; it is the higher heart chakra situated between the throat chakra and the heart chakra. If you thump firmly on the thymus three times (without hurting the person of course) and say *"ha, ha, ha"* three times (nine in all) this should improve the energetic flow and give an uplifting feeling.

21. Mental and Emotional Causes of Disease

In order to heal we first need to intend to get better, and some people would rather take potions and pills than face the repressed emotions that healing can bring to the surface. Some enjoy the attention that they receive as a result of being ill; this can mean that their inner child is craving love or that they are just lonely. Others may be stuck in a victim mentality level of consciousness, which means that they are happy moaning and blaming the world for their illness or problems as it takes the responsibility for correcting the situation off their own shoulders. Whatever the case may be, it is important to realise that illness can teach us so much, usually the hard way unfortunately, through pain and suffering.

Your soul chooses certain diseases in order to get your attention and point you in the right direction. Some people prefer surgery rather than changing their negative thinking or behaviour, and that is their choice.

We can only heal when we are ready and we can only help others when they ask us for help, unless we ask permission from their higher selves, of course. Some people sit back and expect God or a doctor to heal them, but by handing over their healing process to their doctor, they are actually giving away their power.

We need to participate in our own healing process and hope that we are on track. Thanking God every day for our health and wellbeing as we begin to heal is a good start. The Native Americans thought that evoking the help of the lizard would help with the regeneration of the physical body, and hence the healing process.

It is also important to have hope, as hopelessness can cause us to shut down completely, and may even cause terminal illness in itself. Hope means we have some kind of faith, and where there is faith there is light, and this is essential to healing, as, after all, we are made of light energy.

People with hope and a positive mental outlook will get better much quicker than those without these attributes. The hope-less ones will either get worse or take longer to get better, and feeling sorry for themselves will only take away their positive healing power.

In order to heal it is important to remove the energy blocks from the body. These are usually repressed mental and emotional feelings and belief systems, all of which are masses of energy that have formed to create an ailment over a period of time. They are negative programming, but all energy can be moved and transformed. Hatred, anger, fear, jealously, for example, can all be released and replaced with purer energy.

Most people are scared of facing these repressed emotions, but once they do they usually find that it was not as bad as they thought it was going to be, and they can then move on with their lives with a sense of peace and freedom as well as a healthy body. Miracles happen every day; it's just that the people who perform them usually do not feel the need to shout about it.

There are many ways to find help and healing; our human body is a self-healing machine; once pointed in the right direction, it can regenerate on many levels. Think how quickly the skin heals after a nasty case of sunburn, or how a cut finger or limb knits together and heals. We see scars heal and stitches removed after operations only days after we have had them. It is miraculous how quickly we can heal.

Once you realise that the body self heals, you just need to find some way of helping yourself to release the repressed negative and emotional memories that have caused the physical problems, and then you will be on the path to health and wellbeing again.

Ask for help from your angels, or guides, or whatever you believe in. Find the right therapist. Ask your friends. Make sure your therapists realise that they are only a guide and not in control of the healing. I never heal my clients; I help them to heal themselves by moving the blocks. A therapist can open the door but you are the one that walks through it, and a little faith goes a long, long way.

There are many different reasons for illness and disease, but listed here are a few of the most common ones that I have come across.

Migraines
These can be related to frustration, or an overload of information, also repressed rage. They are also a way of taking time out for some people, and possibly in a few cases, attention seeking. Other causes include anger, perfectionism and sugar. These are all factors that should be addressed.

Ears
Problems with your ears relate to not wanting to hear what is going on in the world; we are shutting down to things that we don't like the sound of. Earaches, especially in young children, can mean that they are not happy in their environment. Deafness is about not wanting to listen to other people and not wanting to hear what they are saying. Tinnitus is related to not expressing enough self-love as your soul shuts the outside world out as it forces us to focus upon ourselves.

Neck
Problems here can reflect an inflexible attitude to life, as the head and body become separated, leading us to become materialist and shallow. A blocked chakra can also cause throat problems, with stiff necks being about restricted vision and not seeing all sides of the story (narrow-mindedness). Stress can also lead to neck problems.

Back
Upper back and shoulder problems are related to needing some emotional support, with feeling burdened and carrying the weight of the world on

our shoulders, and often concerns about money. Problems in the middle back can be related to guilt, fear and anger, which can get trapped in the kidneys and cause pain. The lower back is usually around the location of the sacral chakra (just below the naval) which is the emotional centre and can mean holding on to unexpressed emotions that need to be let out. Problems with the root, or the base of the spine, can also relate to not being grounded, or even the lack of will to live.

Stomach

This is the point of power in the body. Problems here seem to stem from who, or what, we can stomach. Fear also causes problems in this area. If this area is blocked, the result is a lack of focus. It is about digesting reality and feelings.

Ulcers

These are related to fear, and feeling we are not good enough, low self-esteem, and other self-worth issues.

Bladder

Infections here are connected to holding in painful emotions, and being 'peed off' with what is going on around us.

Prostate

Problems in this area are related to issues with self-worth and sexual prowess, and are much more common in older men than younger men.

Knees

Problems here can indicate issues with authority, or the fear of moving forward. They can also indicate emotional problems. Knee pain can be due to blocked energy centres causing problems with grounding. Other issues might be that we are too proud, or we are resistant to moving into a new direction.

Gout
This can relate to holding on to negative emotions, thought patterns and attitudes. This can be due to a lack of good blood flow related to lack of love flowing through us and hence not enough energy to balance the negative feelings.

Cancer
Amongst many other potential causes, this can be related to an accumulation of negative emotional and mental energy in the affected area. It appears to be the manifestation of years of negative feelings and emotions on a deep level.

Take breast cancer for example. This can be related to a lack of self-love. Women have more problems with self-love than men do, because women are often seen as someone's wife, mother, daughter, etc, instead of being seen as a woman in their own right and being seen as themselves. Being all these things to all these people and constantly giving to others, closes them to giving to themselves, which can lead to lymph tissue problems. These are connected to the thymus gland, the higher heart chakra. Blocked lymph nodes are common and can be cleared by having a lymphatic massage.

Then you need to love yourself, and I mean really love yourself. It is not selfish, can be life saving, and is essential. After all, you want to live long enough to see your children grow up and to be around for your family, so you will not only be doing yourself a favour by putting yourself first, but you will be prolonging your life, and that will benefit them. If you do not love yourself your thymus chakra can become blocked, thereby blocking the underarm lymph glands, which can affect the lymphatic system and cause disease.

Self-love and creative expression are such important parts of being a woman, or a man for that matter. We all need to love and accept ourselves more, and here a few ways we can do it:

a. Treat yourself to some flowers or goodies every now and then.
b. Take some time out to do exactly what you want on a regular basis.
c. Have a glass of wine now, but remember the first glass can be healthy, whereas the second glass cancels out the first and the third glass is toxic.

d. Say *"NO"* more often, especially to your family, otherwise they can take, take, take, if you let them. I am sure you realise that.
e. Delegate some of the chores. You are not a servant.
f. Have a weekend off, go away in the country every now and then. They will survive without you, honest.
h. Ask for help when you need it, instead of trying to do it all by yourself. It is important to stop giving all the time. This allows for some balance in allowing yourself to receive—give and take. Most of all, do not feel guilty about having some 'me' time. We all deserve it. Try not to worry about your family, as it only sends them negative energy, which will do them and you more harm than good. Look after yourself more and you will live a much longer and happier life.

I once read a little book by Mike George called *'The 7 Aha!s of Highly Enlightened Souls'* in which he stated that research scientists had taken Serotonin, a chemical hormone produced in the human brain when we are happy, and placed it in a test tube with cancer cells in. The cancer cells were killed immediately. When they were asked why they had not tried this before, the scientists replied that there were a million chemicals that needed to be tested and they had only just got round to trying Serotonin. Perhaps that experiment proves that happiness can heal disease, maybe even cancer.

When we look at common ailments then think about the mental, emotional or even spiritual causes, we can see how important it is to release our fears, speak our truths and to put ourselves first, not in a conceited way, and to love ourselves, in order to be loved.

Not speaking our truth means that we hold emotions and negativity in, and this can lead to all kinds of illness. Not loving ourselves leaves us open to abusive partners, heart and lung problems and low self-worth. It is so important to be good to yourself and deal with issues, as they arise if possible. Bottling things up causes stress in the body, and can kill you if you allow this to persist.

22. *Disease and Cell Memory*

Most of us are already aware that the human body has the ability to rejuvenate itself, allowing it to self-heal. The organs and cells all rejuvenate at different speeds. The eyes take approximately two days, the liver takes six weeks, and we have new skin every three to four weeks. With this knowledge, you might ask the question *"Why do we still have cancer in the organs if they are replaced through this rejuvenation?"*

The answer is related to cell memory. Cells in the human body have a memory, or blueprint, that is passed on from the old cell to the new cell when it rejuvenates. Each old cell passes on the exact information necessary for that cell to replicate the original, even if it is diseased; thus passing on the memory of, let us say, the cancer.

It is possible to break this chain by finding the initial cause of the cell memory problem, the issue that caused the cell to turn cancerous. This could be the result of an emotional or mental trauma some time ago—for instance, a particular incident that triggered the first cell to turn cancerous.

I believe, as do many others, that we have the ability to find out that information by connecting to that inner wisdom and then working towards harmony to remove the cause of the disease. In my experience it is possible to find this information fairly easily by working with the inner wisdom of the human body. This is the same wisdom that keeps us breathing when we sleep, and knows the function of every cell. When we know what the cause was, we can hopefully rectify that and cure the problem.

This wisdom can be reached via connection to the higher self, as explained in Chapter 26 'Connecting with your Higher Self.' Finding the cause is quite often the easy bit. Next, you need to remove the memory by removing the hurtful emotions, sadness, anger, fear, etc. This can be difficult for some, as they would rather not revisit the painful experience, however temporarily. However, it is important to sometimes go back in order to go forward, and it is an important part of the healing process.

The way to access the cause is to connect with your higher self and take your conscious awareness into, say, a tumour, by setting the intention in your mind that you are inside the tumour, or imagining you can see it in your mind's eye. Then ask your higher self or inner wisdom what caused the tumour to grow, and even what will help to dissipate it, and just sit quietly and wait for the answer to come into your mind, and to trust the process.

This usually leads back to some sort of emotional upset, and the next part of the process involves working through the issues and forgiving either yourself or the other person completely. Many of my clients have found the answers to why they have cancer using this technique, and this gives them the opportunity to work on releasing the particular issue, or to carry out the lifestyle changes needed to heal themselves.

Writing—but not sending—a letter to the person can also help; the letter allows a release of the emotions onto the page, and then the letter is burnt to transmute the energy. I also occasionally take people through a meditation to discuss the issues with the other person on a soul level, which can be very helpful. Once the emotional or mental issue has been released, it is necessary to work on the physical. If the tumour has not been removed by surgery, I would work on it using visualisation techniques as discussed in Chapter 7: 'Heal Thyself,' which explains the visualisation I used on my own damaged cells. The visualisation can be adapted to suit the way you see things.

Many natural remedies help with illness and can complement medical treatment. Sometimes we will find a soul fragment as part of the healing, especially with childhood traumas (see Chapter 33 about Soul Retrieval).

It is important to realise that people who hurt us are helping us to learn about life, and are a necessary part of our journey and our Karma. Even though it seems unfair, we should try to let go of blame, as well as forgiving them and ourselves. We need to infuse love into every situation to reach the point of freedom from the stresses caused by holding on to the past. Letting go is very important and can take time. My advice is keep at it. You will get there eventually.

23. *Fear*

Fear is a basic survival emotion and is connected to the base chakra, which is related to our fight or flight instinct. All forms of fear are protective instincts and should not be ignored, as fear moves us away from danger and relates to self-preservation. Equally, fear should not be pandered to either.

As you now know, like attracts like, so fearful emotions may attract fearful energies. These negative energies are attracted to fear-based emotions such as anger, bitterness or rage, jealousy and vengefulness, for example. We all get angry now and again, and usually that emotion will quickly dissipate. What causes problems is being in an angry state for a long time. Long-term anger can attract dark energies, spirits and entities that are drawn, as if to a magnet, to negative emotional energy.

As I mentioned earlier, I recently discovered that I had hidden fears regarding fear of attack and also a fear of invasion by ET's. This was because I had watched Sci-fi movies as a child and even though I really enjoyed them, they planted negative seeds in a vulnerable mind. This put me at risk of attracting low frequency extraterrestrials in this time line, as we attract the things that are within our sub conscious mind. The human mind absorbs everything and because the sub conscious cannot distinguish between what is real and what is fantasy, I highly recommend clearing your mind of these fears, especially if you watched movies like this. Think how even watching something as entertaining as Dr Who, may have planted sub-conscious fears in you and your family. For this reason, I am very careful about what I watch and read; the purer your mind, the purer your world.

Violence of any type is very good at attracting very low-frequency energies. Long-term repressed negative emotions can, after a while, turn into a certain type of entity. These can feel dense, and look like a black mass of energy. Some may even have tentacles, looking more like something from the abyss, or a science-fiction movie. I once removed one of these black energies, the size of a car wheel. It had tentacles about 2-3 inches thick. It was attached to the wound of a woman who was in the intensive care unit of my local hospital, having contracted a killer bug, similar to MRSA, but called necrotising fasciitis; it literally eats your flesh away and can kill you within 24 hrs. She only went into hospital for keyhole surgery to be sterilised, and ended up at death's door. She was in hospital for seven weeks in total. Thank God she survived, but she does have serious scarring on her body, as a result of much of the dead flesh having been cut away in order to save her life.

This made me think that maybe these 'bugs,' so to speak, are really entities that are attracted to the sick and vulnerable. In this context, the term 'entity' means a mass of invisible energy, good or bad. It is not something from a horror movie, just bad energy and can easily be removed.

This was not the first time I had seen and removed one of these black masses from a person in hospital. On another occasion a woman had a brain tumour, and the mass was wrapped around her head. Was it attracted to her negative thinking, did it affect the growth of the tumour or maybe it was responsible for the tumour, and had been there for a long period of time? Who knows? I have my opinion but you may want to draw your own conclusions.

Drugs and alcohol (and by alcohol I mean more than one glass of wine) affect us in a negative manner. When we get 'high' or drunk, our crown chakra opens and we become vulnerable to all sorts of negative energies or entities, and we can even become possessed. Yes, I did say possessed. Consider this for a moment: when was the last time you heard a person say *"I don't know what possessed me to do that"*, after they have behaved out of character after one too many drinks.

These negative energies can pop into you, making you take leave of your senses, and then exit again, leaving you to clean up their mess. Worse, they can move into your body and stay, causing all sorts of problems, from personality changes, alcoholism or even chronic fatigue, and at the very worst, suicide.

If you think this may have happened to someone you know, you can ask their permission to do the tie-cutting techniques and energy clearing described elsewhere in this book, which should help. I believe this will help lots of people, especially ones with health issues such as chronic fatigue. Clearing the negative clouds of energy from the mental layer of the aura, and clearing the crown chakra will elevate their thinking to a higher level, creating a more positive mindset.

Smoking can also cause problems related to negative energies. One evening I decided to visit an old friend of mine on the way home from work. The house was full of girls getting ready for a wild night out on the town, a birthday party. They were all drinking wine and some were smoking. I had given up smoking about 18 months before but did have a cigarette now and then, as I found it easy not to have a second one and just stop again. With this cigarette I also had a glass of wine. Before I left to go home, my friend, by this point a bit worse for wear, gave me a hug.

The repercussions were immediate and terrible. I felt as if I had been hit in the chest and stomach with a hammer. It was a mighty bang, and it left me feeling weak and sick. With my heart racing, I had to go straight home, wondering what on earth had happened to make me feel so ill. It was as if I had been violated in some way.

During that night I was woken by 'alarm bells' going off in my sleep. In my mind's eye I could see that I had a huge 'V' shape hole in my aura. I was wide open. The energetic wiring in my body (my meridians) had been chopped and ripped up.

I began repairing it by pulling the edges in and weaving it back together with rays of light from my fingertips. Using visualisation techniques, I reconnected each wire and fused them back together until every wire was fixed. I did a tie-cutting, and could see a dark shadow around me that must have been attached to my friend, and when she had hugged me it contaminated me. One cigarette had caused this problem, opening holes in my aura and allowing the shadow in. It was my own fault and I paid severely for that smoke. Smoking and alcohol are not acceptable when you reach a certain level of attainment, as they are considered to be self-sabotage, and will block your spiritual growth. I understand that now. Sobriety is the wise choice.

The Universe will allow someone, or something, in to sabotage you if you self-sabotage. Try to remember that. As your level of attainment becomes higher, you will find that even eating the wrong foods can be considered self-sabotage. If you feel you are being attacked or sabotaged, have a good look to see what you are doing to create this situation yourself, before you start to blame others.

When we are under the influence of drugs or alcohol, holes open up in our aura, and we have a weakened energy field as a result. When these energies get hold we need to clear them as soon as possible, and tie-cutting and energy clearing can be instigated, with the clear intention that the disc of Crystal Ki light is to clear negative energies, emotions and entities, and to clear any negativity from the aura and from all levels of consciousness.

Your intention is very important. For example if the issue is anger, then work on removing that; if the emotion is fear, then focus on clearing that. Name the specific emotion when you set your intentions at the beginning of the tie-cutting and energy clearing exercise in this book.

Simple breathing exercises can help to release fear, visualising the fear leaving on the out breath. To do this sit in a quiet place, breathe in slowly as you count to five, then hold your breath for five seconds, then breathe out for five seconds. See the fear leave your body with the out breath, and imagine that every bit of fear is being released. Practise this over and again for at least fifteen minutes and it will help to release the fear, and also aid relaxation.

24. *Forgive them for you, not them!*

Forgiveness is very important to our health and wellness and is a vital part of the healing process. We can be tied to someone we are in conflict with for lifetimes, if we refuse to forgive them. Healing is not achieved by trying to correct the other person for hurting you, but by realising that all hurt is self-inflicted. We bring it all to our own door.

We create our own karma and therefore we can really only trust God 100%, as anyone else can let us down by delivering negative karma. Trust is naïve when you understand karma. Naïve trust is co-dependency, and this is always a problem. You can trust your husband or best friend but knowing what you do about karma and the illusion of the self-created hologram we see as our 3D world, consider this: let's say that you trust your husband or wife 100%; you have been with them for years. Then all of a sudden they betray you and run off with someone else. Why? Karma and lessons, that's why.

You may need to learn about how to handle betrayal, and that is the way the Universe enables this lesson to work. Maybe you betrayed them in a past life and your Karma has been delivered right back to you. It is important to see that they are just a part of the illusion being projected to deliver your karma, in order to work off karmic debt and to see how you respond. Often it's a test and the wise choice is passive.

The whole point is to learn to forgive and to accept that the betrayal was created by your soul, not the betrayer. Your soul chose this experience, as it chooses all of your experiences, in order for you to learn and grow. The person who betrayed you was just delivering your lesson, or karma.

We must all learn to forgive in order to evolve, and the following exercise may help you to forgive those who have hurt you in the past.

Six Steps to Forgiveness

The following exercise involves six simple steps to forgiveness and having used it myself in the past, I can recommend it as it really helped me. First find a quiet place where you will not be disturbed. You will need a pen and some paper.

1. Write down why you are upset or angry.
2. Write down the good things about the person or people who hurt you.
3. Write down how you contributed to the argument or problem—and be honest!
4. Think about the law of reflection (see Chapter 39 on the Universal Spiritual Law). Reflect on what you have written, whilst looking at all three lists. Think about the person and their importance in your life. How important they are to you may have an effect on the relationship after you have forgiven them. Remember that you are forgiving them for your own needs and spiritual growth. The important thing is to have a good think when you are calm, and the initial anger has dissipated. This may take you a little time. It does not matter; what matters is forgiveness for the sake of your own peace and well-being. You can help by using the space clearing process in the chapter on tie-cutting to clear your anger, by setting that intention. If you feel you should let go of the relationship altogether, that's fine. After you forgive them, tie cut and move on. If you want to carry on with the relationship or friendship, great! That's also fine.

5. State out loud that you forgive them. You may not be able to forget, but you can forgive and let go of the pain and anger. You are healing yourself by forgiving them. You are putting a stop to the negative thoughts running through your mind, which if you hold on to them could damage you and can lead to serious illness. Unforgiveness gets stored in the heart chakra, and can cause the heart to become diseased.
6. Sit quietly and breathe out all of the anger and pain, and visualise it leaving your body in the out breath. You should feel better after this; you do not even have to discuss this with the person.

If you feel you still have not quite let go enough, have a think about what is being reflected back to you. What is the universe trying to show you here? Read the law of reflection in the spiritual law chapter (Chapter 39) again, and then go back to step 4 above, and think about it a little longer. Once you are happy and feel you have forgiven them, you can burn the papers as this helps transform the energy.

This may appear to be a pointless exercise but it really does help. Try it and find out!

25. *The Chakras and Auric Bodies*

The chakras and the auric bodies are perceived as the energetic systems of a human being. Chakras are cone-shaped vortices of light shaped like a small tornado with the point of the cone connecting to the main channel which runs down the spine from the crown to the base. These energy centres are described as spinning wheels of light, varying in colour, depending upon their frequency and position. They directly relate to mental, emotional, physical and spiritual health. These energy centres are interconnected, working in unison, and in balancing one, you will affect the others.

Most books relate to seven chakras but I tend to work on twelve—ten in the body, with one above the head (higher crown), and one below the feet (earth star chakra). The eight main chakras radiate out from the main channel running down the spinal column forming the vertical axis. There are hundreds of other smaller chakras each connected to an acupressure or an acupuncture point.

Viewed from the front, a healthy chakra will be brightly coloured and spinning clockwise, whereas an unhealthy chakra will be dull, and if it is trying to clear itself, it will be spinning counter-clockwise. These energy centres respond to all forms of stimuli and pass on the messages they receive to the internal organs and the physical body as a whole. They affect everything and can become unbalanced by our lifestyle, mental attitude, sexual behaviour, and our emotional and physical activities. Even the colour of the food we eat can affect the chakras. That is why it is good to have many colours of food on your plate and to eat plenty of greens, as green is the colour of the heart chakra.

The chakras are what keep us alive and keep us in our physical form, and without them we would not be here; it is therefore vital that we care for these energy centres. As we raise our vibration we cleanse and clear these chakras, and wake up to a higher level of awareness as a result, especially when we balance the crown chakra and learn to connect to our higher selves.

Problems can begin way out in the auric bodies and filter down through the layers and can eventually cause disease in the physical body. The aura is a bio-energetic sheath covering the whole physical body and is made up of many different layers. We will discuss seven of these.

As well as emotional and mental energies affecting the chakras, we may have etheric blocks I refer to as Soul Implants. These are placed in us before we incarnate to stop us raising our consciousness too quickly and blowing our fuses, so to speak. There may also be extraterrestrial chips and transmitters in our bodies that can cause problems too. For more information, see Diagrams 1 and 2 in Book 2 *'Saving the World from my Bathtub'*. I teach students how to remove these things in my workshops.

During the last 2500 years of the Piscean Age people primarily worked on one body, or at the most two or three bodies. We now need to cleanse and develop all of these bodies to achieve the necessary unity for utilising the power of Aquarian Age energies. One aspect of the Aquarian Age is increased awareness of the physical body and its functions. Most of us have been trained to rely primarily on our brainpower for information, but by tuning into the consciousness received by the body through the chakras, we will become more in tune with higher mental and spiritual energies, free from restrictions and brain programming. Development and use of the brain was very important in the Piscean Age, but now we also need to expand to higher octaves of mental and spiritual energies.

All healing and ascension processes work towards integrating our spiritual light body into our lower physical body. We bring the new energies down to us and anchor them into our energetic bodies; we do not go up to join with them, as the word ascension suggests.

In order to fully integrate your light body (your Merkaba) you will need to reactivate your dormant DNA. It is possible to reactivate your DNA by visiting a practitioner who knows how to do this, or by using prayer and meditation. Simply set your intention to connect with God, the First Creator, and ask him to begin to reactivate your higher strands of DNA, NOW!

Then use either the tie-cutting techniques or prayer to remove any etheric implants that may be blocking DNA functionality. A simple prayer to God, the First Creator asking him to remove all implants, NOW! Make sure that you say "NOW" with meaning.

Then brace yourself, as the energy can shift very quickly through your body. I am informed that it is possible to reactivate as many as twelve strands of DNA in as little as three months.

In Book 4: *'The Avatar & the Crystal Key'* I list the first 58 strands of our DNA. There are many more strands to be activated as we evolve!

We should open our minds safely to higher level of consciousness, but not too quickly, as it can literally blow the mind and damage the nervous system.

The purpose of this healing is to clear your endocrine and hormonal systems, allowing your light body to be aligned throughout your chakra system, allowing for ascension through the process of raising your vibration.

I use grids of light to cleanse the chakras and reprogram the cell memory and it works well; others use mantras and meditation. These changes affect the endocrine and hormonal systems. The endocrine system monitors everything within the physical body. It monitors and adjusts, regulating and maintaining the correct functioning of your organs at a cellular level. It also has a primary function of connecting the lower physical energies to the higher spiritual energies.

Once these changes take place, more energy can flow via the DNA strands, the chakras, the endocrine and the hormonal systems. As they are restored to their primary purpose we are more fully able to recognise the Christ consciousness within each and every one of us.

This may all sound very complicated, but the sub-conscious can be reprogrammed in a matter of minutes. I do this at the end of treatments with clients who are at the correct level of consciousness and are ready for the process to be carried out. It can transform their lives by removing negative patterns on a deep subconscious level.

The Auric Bodies (Bio- energetic sheath)
(see Diagram 1 below)

Physical Body
The physical body is the densest of the seven bodies, the only one that can be seen without clairvoyant vision. With the physical body, we express, we receive, and we become aware.

Emotional Body
The emotional body has a vibratory rate through which we feel and express emotions; it is also a passageway to the divine, and when fully developed, serves as an outlet for feelings of divine love.

Mental Body

The mental body is the vibratory rate through which we think and reason. When we operate in the lower levels of the mental body, our thoughts and attitudes may be heavily influenced by feelings, giving rise to 'desire mind', products of which include prejudices, opinions and other forms of emotional thinking. Operating at higher levels of the mental body we are capable of abstract thinking, creativity, logical reasoning, mathematics and philosophy.

Intuitional/Compassionate Body

This is a vibratory rate where one feels compassion, and understanding of self and others. It is also a vehicle for the expression of higher forms of love; a gateway to the Divine, serving as a connecting link between the emotional and the divine levels. In this body, we are beyond the limits of time and space; there is understanding without the need to go through a process of reasoning and thinking. This is the home of intuition.

Will/Spirit Body

The Will/Spirit body is the vehicle, or vibratory rate, through which spirit expresses. It channels energy that manifests as will, and is said to be the highest level a person can reach and still negate the Divine or Soul levels; because the energy is so high, this brings the potential for great negativity or karma. This is the area for choice, Divine will, or individual will.

Soul Body

The soul body is the vehicle for the expression of soul energies, where one experiences self as one with God, self-experienced as a unit of God's consciousness.

Divine Body

In this seventh body we relate to the spark of the divine within us. We can deeply feel the presence of God in our lives and feel oneness with a divine reality.

Chakras and Colours

Chakra colours mean various things. I have listed the original colours and meanings below:

Red	Passion, life energy
Orange	Creativity and feminine energy
Yellow	Wisdom and power and intellect
Green / Pink	Healing and Love
Aquamarine	Unconditional love
Turquoise blue	Communication
Indigo blue	Intuition and guidance
Purple / White	Vision and spirituality
Silver	The transference of energy and a clear human connection to the divine
Gold	Soul purpose and harmony
Pearl White	Source Energy

New colours are now coming through from the Universe that are much more opalescent in appearance. They include a pinkie-orange, a lime green, a petrol blue, a deep royal purple, aquamarine and a deep, dark pink.

The Chakras
(see Diagrams 1 and 2 below, I have shown only fourteen but there are many more)

The Stellar Gateway (Gold)
This is depicted as a tunnel of pure light or a portal that connects the soul to the Divine Source. Activation and clearing of this chakra opens a cosmic doorway to all of the Light Densities, and enhances communication with Enlightened Beings that exist in the Densities of Light beyond the physical worlds. Its purpose is to maintain a link between the creator and creation. It is through this chakra that highly spiritual humans will experience ultimate consciousness. Accessing this centre can be detrimental to the mental health unless the person is ready and spiritually evolved.

Soul Star (White)
It is through this Higher Crown chakra that the soul braids into the physical at the time of incarnation (birth), and it is through this chakra that the soul leaves the physical body upon death. Access to the Soul Star chakra increases direct contact with the soul, and the communication of the soul's intent is enhanced.

The Causal Chakra (Silver)
This important vortex lies at the outer edge of the aura and regulates the flow of energy from the Soul Star Chakra to the body. In practice, it regulates Soul-braiding and enables the physical body to attune to the increased energy of Soul Consciousness, and to the Higher Density Light existence resulting from the Soul-braiding. The Causal chakra is the centre that accepts the 'dosages' of light that the upper two chakras deliver, and assists in higher activations of the Crown, Brow and Throat chakras.

Crown Chakra
(**Violet**)—Associated with enlightenment, meanings of life and existence.

(**Shimmering golden white**)—associated with the state of perfection in mind, body, emotions and spirituality. It is the most purely spiritual chakra. It is through this centre that we gain wisdom from the spirit realm and the connection to cosmic consciousness. When clear, we are able to see through the illusion, we become self-aware and can consciously detach from personal emotions. It vitalises the cerebrum, right eye and the pineal gland. Once activated the process of realising 'who we are' begins. It governs the upper brain and the pineal gland. It facilitates connection to the higher self, inner guidance, the higher levels of consciousness, oneness, unconditional love, spiritual awareness, intuition and wisdom. It is the main entry point for our incarnation and life force. When blocked, we feel weak and low.

Brow Chakra (Indigo)
Associated with attainment, the pursuit for our spiritual purpose in life, the Third Eye is located above the eyebrows in the middle of the forehead.

It is the centre of psychic power, psychic vision, higher intuition, spiritual energies, magnetic forces and light. When activated, one's perception of life will alter for the better. This chakra allows access to higher information via intuition and the connection to outside guidance. It helps to release negative tendencies and selfish attitudes. It governs the lower left brain, left eye, nose, ears, spine, pituitary gland, face, central nervous system and the production of hormones. It is the centre of will, inner vision, thought control, inspiration, clairvoyance and spiritual awakening. This chakra is interconnected to the Sacral chakra.

Throat Chakra   (Blue)

Associated with knowledge of the Oneness with Divine guidance, located at the centre of the throat. We are able to look at multiple perspectives when this centre is activated. It is the centre of communication, sound and expression of creativity via thought, speech and writing. It is the centre of openness, creativity, judgement, self-expression a sense of responsibility, and the ability to hear other peoples' opinions and points of view. It governs the throat, thyroid, four para-thyroids, bronchial, oesophagus, vocal chords, neck, arms, digestive tract, lungs, jaws and cheeks. This centre vitalises the breath and the body's metabolic rate.

Thymus chakra/Higher Heart Chakra   (Aquamarine)

This chakra represents our protection of ourselves. It is the filter between the head and the heart. It is located between the throat and the heart, linked to the immune system. An imbalance here can show itself as HIV/Aids, auto-immune disorders and recurrent viral/bactericidal illness, glandular fever, lymphatic blockages, and repeated colds and coughs that can be difficult to shake off. It governs loving communication, and when balanced, you may notice that you are not allowing negative people to affect you so much, you are not catching every virus that comes along, and your emotions are felt deeply and released quickly. Where the heart chakra radiates human love, the Thymus chakra or Higher Heart, as it is also referred to, radiates unconditional love and the Christ/Buddha consciousness.

Heart Chakra

(Pink)—Associated with softness, compassion, empathy and pure emotions such as love. The primary function of the heart chakra is to link the higher levels of consciousness to the physical; it is the astral bridge. Its secondary function is the expression of love of self and others.

(Green)—Associated with healing, ecstasy and exhilaration. It is located in the centre of the chest. This is the centre of love, spirituality and, with the 'Oneness' of the Universe, compassion and group consciousness. It vitalises the heart, lungs, thymus, blood system, cellular structure, skin and hands. It is the centre for emotions—sympathy, selflessness, trust, spiritual development, forgiveness, devotion, peace and healing. Most healers work through their Heart chakras, and if you find a good one, their Higher Heart too. You can feel the difference when you are with someone who has their Higher Heart chakra functioning. They radiate a beautiful energy, which is very uplifting and peaceful.

Solar Plexus   (Yellow)

Associated with meditative, analytical thought and intellectual activity. It is located below the breastbone. This centre is the store of Ki (Universal life force) and personal power, ambition, intellect, strength, fear, jealousy, loss of love, tolerance, wisdom, inner calm, peace, and acceptance of others. It vitalises the stomach, liver, gall bladder, spleen, large and small intestines, sympathetic nervous system, pancreas and adrenal glands. Each of the body's organs deals with a certain emotion, e.g. liver—jealousy and fear; kidneys—fear; spleen—anger.

Sacral Chakra   (Orange)

Associated with wisdom, creativity and benevolence to all. It is located approximately two inches below the navel at the pelvis just below the junction with the spine. Lots of people get pain in the lower back due to old repressed emotions. A good cry will help release the tension in this area. It is this centre that governs the digestive system and the reproductive organs. It is attuned to emotions and thoughts concerning wellness. The Sacral chakra is linked to the Brow chakra and, when balanced, it assists in the development of psychic skills. It is the zone of vitality, enjoyment, self-esteem, awe, sensuality, eroticism, enthusiasm and relationships. Its primary function is creativity. Its secondary function is sexual relationships and sexual activity, the latter remaining dormant until puberty, which then stimulates the onset of hormonal changes in the body.

Base or Root Chakra

(Black)—Associated with stability and grounding to the source of security located at the base of the spine. Black has all of the colours of the rainbow in it, and should not be feared. Black crystals are very grounding.

(Red)—Associated with the essential, idealistic and confident passion for life. It is linked to kundalini, psychic potential, adrenal glands, teeth, nails, anus, legs, kidneys, urinary system, skin, muscles, blood, intestines, prostate gland, bladder, bones and skeletal structure. It is the centre of vitality, physical energy and self-preservation. It is the zone of fight or flight. Many people have an imbalance here, because the fight or flight response is not allowed to be acted upon. Fighting is socially unacceptable and so is running away.

Knee Chakras (Maroon)

The Knee chakras are minor chakras governing movement, and are the gateway for grounding the soul into form. Most knee problems are a result of the energy becoming turned off from the knee down to the feet. Working on the knees allows the energy to flow freely down to the feet and Earth Star chakra. The Knee chakra governs strength of purpose and our sense of worthiness. It governs the shoulder and neck muscles. It also monitors the flow of the body's energies.

Feet Chakras (Brown)

The Feet chakras govern balance, wholeness and the logic mind. They regulate the flow of the body's energy from the physical layer to the spiritual layer. The Feet chakras are minor chakras, but are nonetheless important, regarding our connection to earth and grounding the body's energy. Placing your hands on a client's shoulders causes their Feet chakras to open and thus helps to ground them. Grounding is essential to both the healer and the client.

The Earth Star Chakra   (Dark Brown)
This is located between and slightly below the feet (approximately 12 inches-30cm). It links the physical body to the earth via a vibratory energetic cord that hooks into the earth and holds the etheric bodies and the soul incarnate. It governs bonding, and produces a sense of connectedness and a sense of community.

THE CHAKRAS

THE AURIC BODIES

- The Stellar Gateway
- Soul Star (Higher Crown)
- Causal Chakra
- Crown Chakra
- Brow Chakra (Third Eye Chakra)
- Throat Chakra
- Thymus Chakra (Higher Heart Chakra)
- Heart Chakra
- Solar Plexus Chakra
- Sacral Chakra
- Base Chakra (Root Chakra)
- Knee Chakras
- Feet Chakras
- Earth Star Chakra

Divine body (Ketheric Body) (Mental aspect)

Soul Body / Celestial Body (Emotional aspect)

Will/Spirit Body / Etheric Template (physical aspect)

Intuitional/Compassionate Body / Astral Body

Mental Body (Lower mental aspect)

Emotional Body (Lower emotional aspect)

Physical Etheric Body (Lower etheric aspect)

Spiritual plane

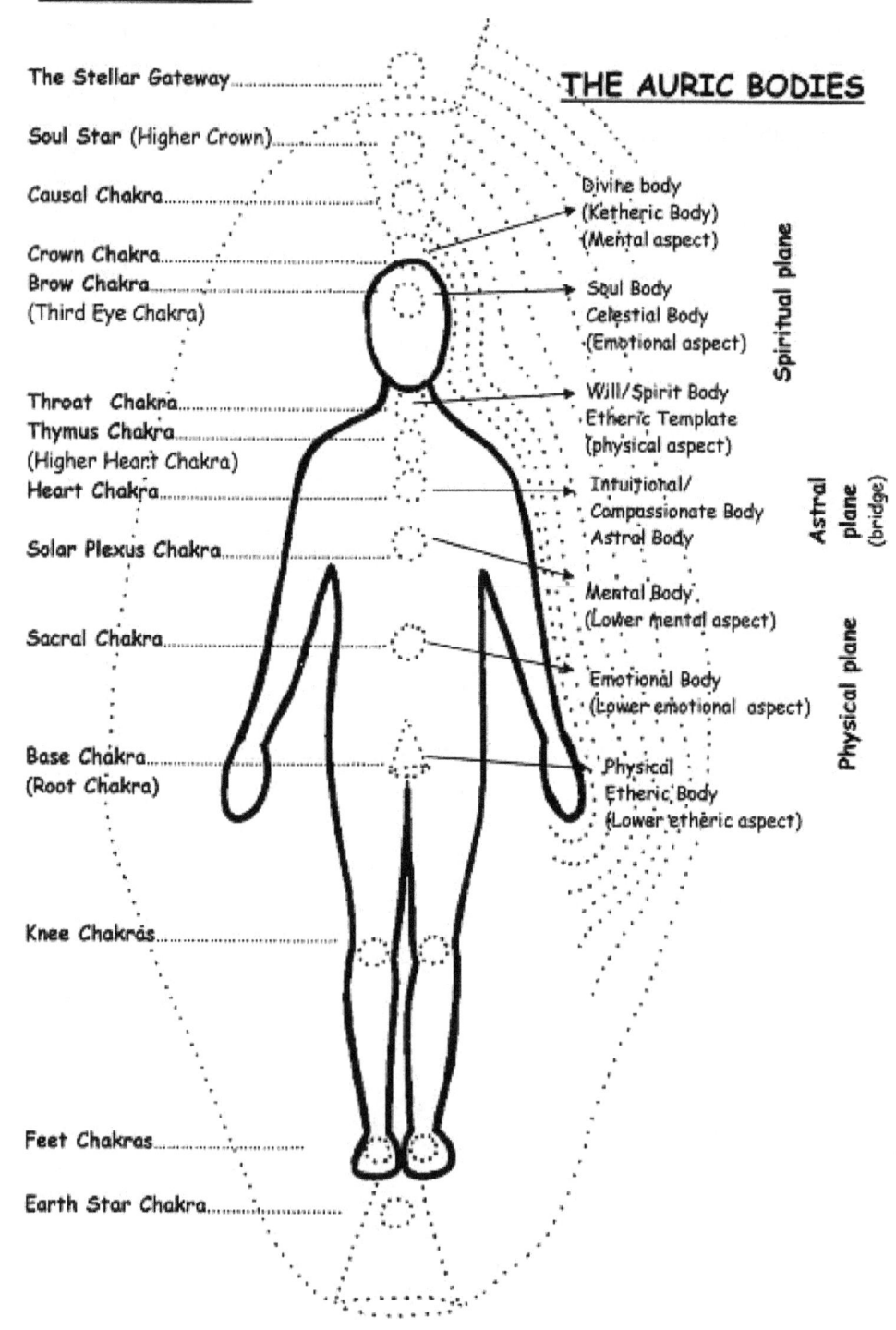

Astral plane (bridge)

Physical plane

Diagram 1 - Adapted from Barbara Ann Brennan's - Hands of Light

Main Chakras (Side View)

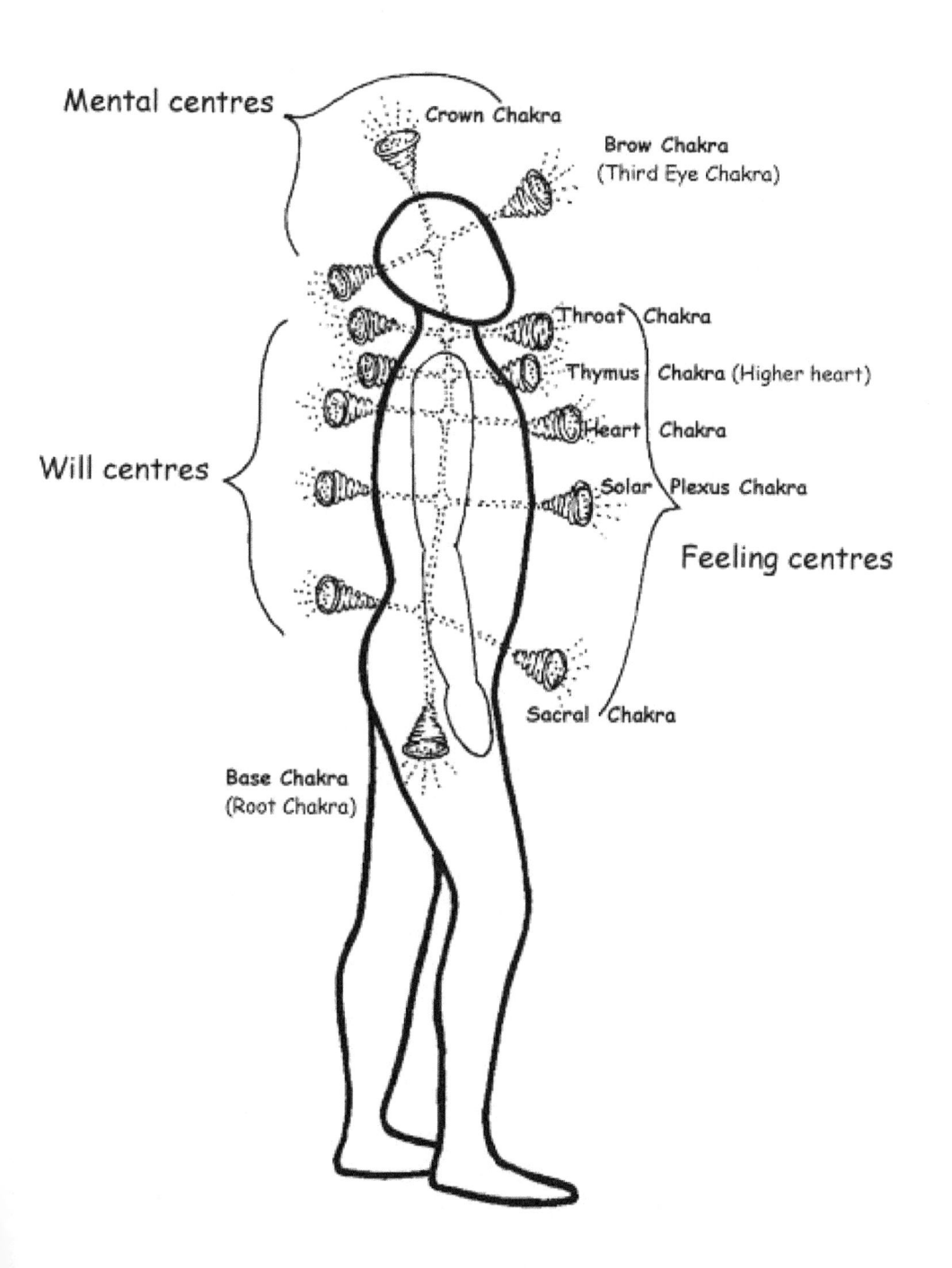

Mental centres
- Crown Chakra
- Brow Chakra (Third Eye Chakra)
- Throat Chakra
- Thymus Chakra (Higher heart)
- Heart Chakra
- Solar Plexus Chakra

Will centres

Feeling centres

- Sacral Chakra
- Base Chakra (Root Chakra)

Diagram 2 - Adapted from Barbara Ann Brennan's - Hands of Light

26. Connecting to your Higher Self

Learning how to connect to your higher self is a useful exercise from which you can find out all sorts of valuable information from a higher level of consciousness.

Before you start working with your higher self, it is important to ensure that you are grounded. Do this by visualising an orb of light of about 1m (3ft) in diameter around your Earth Star chakra, which is about 30cm (12 inches) beneath your feet below the ground.

If you feel the need, camouflage this orb. Camouflaging is useful to hide your light when you are in certain places, as lower frequency energies will not be able to see you as easily.

Then see a connection from the base of your spine going down your legs and out to your feet and connecting to your Earth Star chakra inside that protective orb. Intend and state that this orb is to act as a filter, to purify any negative energies coming into your body from the ground.

I have seen a lot of lower octave energy in the ground that is not for the highest good, and my guidance is to protect myself from it. This technique is one that works very well for me. It is very important to do this, otherwise during meditation and working with the higher mind, you are likely to feel other-worldly, spaced-out, and light-headed, so it is important to ground yourself. Drinking water, and stamping your feet firmly on the floor, are both good ways of helping to ground you.

I would also recommend an energy clearing before you start, to ensure that the information is from your higher self and not any other source. Spirits or other energies can interfere with guidance and they are not always easy to sense. Some negative energies can actually hook into people and drain their energy, or manipulate them via a kind of lead or chain; even people who surround themselves in white light are vulnerable. It is important to be discerning as just because something tells you it is an angel, does not mean that it really is. Personally I believe surrounding yourself in white light is like lighting a candle. It attracts moths. It is safer to ask your higher self to choose the energy that you need to protect you. A tie-cutting and space clearing will remove these unwanted energies.

Once you have grounded and cleared yourself it is safe to begin. Some people find it hard to visualise, or they think that they need to have amazing visual pictures in their mind's eye, but this is not the case. If you find it difficult to visualise, try to imagine it in your mind's eye instead, or sense it with your feelings. It will work just as well as visualising.

The two simple ways to do this are as follows:

1. Visualise a golden orb of light representing your higher self and resting about 30cm (12 inches) above your head. Then see a line of light coming down in through your crown chakra on the top of your head and entering your conscious mind. I see it as a kind of cosmic telephone cable.
2. You can visualise your Christ-self or your Buddha-self, and see that image floating down from above your head and coming into your mind, setting the intention that you are connected to your higher self.

Once you are connected, begin with the following breathing exercises, which will take your brain waves to a more meditative state.

Close your eyes and take a long, slow deep breath in through your nose, filling your whole body with air, allowing your chest and stomach to rise, breathing right down into your abdomen. Then slowly breathe out through your mouth. Repeat this five more times, and feel yourself relaxing more and more with each breath; visualise any stress leaving your body with each out breath.

Take six slow breaths, this time into your lungs only, expanding the chest, breathing in through the nose and out through the mouth.

Now, take six slow breaths into the upper chest only, once again breathing in through the nose and out through the mouth. Allow your breath to find its own natural rhythm.

Now, keeping your eyes closed, just relax for a couple of minutes. Relax and let the information you need come into your mind, and feel the peace flow through your whole body.

When you are finished, drink some water to ground yourself. You might like to set an alarm for 10—15 minutes, in case you fall asleep.

In this semi-meditative state a lot of information can come in very quickly, and so you can begin to ask questions, and the first thing that comes to mind after you have asked a question will be the answer.

I often go through this process with my clients and students, and they will often ask how do they know it's their higher self and not their ego or imagination? I always say that because they have gone through the process of clearing and entering a meditative state, creating the change in brainwaves, will more or less guarantee that the information is coming from their higher self.

Being connected to your higher self is an amazing and powerful tool. You can also use this process to help you become more creative. Let's say, for example, you wanted to paint a picture, write an essay or decorate a room. Before you go to bed just ask your higher self to work on those ideas and to create the images you need whilst you sleep. Let your higher self do some of the work. The next day when you connect with your higher self you can get all of the ideas that came during the night, and then you can put those ideas into practice.

I connect to a higher level of consciousness when I work with my clients, as I like my information to come from my higher consciousness and not my ego self. I do this before I start a treatment, when doing journey work, or any healing work on myself. Being able to make this conscious connection, I know that any information coming to me is from a higher source, a much wiser source, and this has helped me to grow in confidence so much over the years.

27. Crystal Ki Healing Exercises

Of all of the information and meditation exercises I have learned over the years these tie-cutting and energy clearing techniques have proved to be the most useful and powerful, so much so, that they are part of my daily routine.

If you are a healer or therapist and are in contact with people physically during treatments, it is vital that you learn how to cleanse your energy field before and after treatment, for both your sake and theirs. It is possible to pick up attachments from clients and vice versa, so genuine care is needed.

Very early on in my awakening process, I realised that I needed to be free from other people's negative connections to me in order to get to where I was meant to be, even though, at the time, I was not really sure where my spiritual path was leading me. I needed to cut ties with a lot of people, even people I loved dearly, as they were draining my energy. This realisation has been so important, and has helped me to reach a higher level of consciousness. I am eternally grateful to Archangel Michael for helping me with the clearing techniques. He feels more like my elder brother than a celestial being, and I always feel safe because of his presence.

The Tie Cutting and Energy Clearing techniques I teach in my workshops can be used to clear your energy field, the energy in your home or work place, and so on. You can use it on friends and family, even pets and plants. It can be used at a distance, and it will still work just as well if the person is in Australia or in the same room with you.

You must get permission first, always! If you don't, you may suffer the consequences of your pushy, uninvited actions, so I would advise you to use it wisely. All energy work must be carried out with care and attention to detail.

I will explain how the procedure is carried out first, and then give you information in the form of an exercise to use on yourself. I will explain distant clearing, and as you become more familiar with the exercise you can work on remotely. The more you use it on yourself the quicker you will be able to perform the cleansing. I recommend practising it at least once a day for twenty one days. At the end of the twenty one days you should know it by heart and can use it anywhere. I often use it to clear hotel rooms when I am on holiday or at workshops. I like to sleep in a clear space.

I will now explain how to perform the procedure to clear yourself and then give you the exercise in 10 simple steps.

Find a quiet place where you will not be disturbed for at least fifteen minutes. You will need a chair to support your back and a glass of water for after the session.

Generally I like to start by saying a prayer, asking God to guide and protect me and to ensure that all energies that come to me are from God and from no other.

Then invoke the Universal Crystal Ki (CK) healing energies, by saying, *"I call upon the Universal Crystal Ki healing energies and the energies of purification"*. (This is said 3 times).

Next you need to set your intention—this means you need to inform the energies exactly what it is you would like to release and clear. This could be fear, grief, pollution, or even food additives and preservatives that pollute your system.

Once the intention is set, the next step is to carry out some simple breathing exercises, and to imagine your body is inside a sphere of energy. This is your energy field (aura) and for the purpose of this exercise try to imagine it is approximately 5m (16.5 feet) in radius, consisting of 33 layers. This exercise will clear the first 33 layers of your aura, as that is the intention.

Next, imagine a disc of Crystal Ki microscopic diamond energy hovering just above the top of your aura, just outside of it, at level 35. The disc is slightly wider than your energy field and about 1 cm thick.

You need to ask the CK energies to bring it slowly down through your being from level 35 above you, down through your aura, through your physical body, then down through the aura beneath you to level 35 just below the bottom of level 33 of your aura. This disc will loosen any blocks or discordant energies as it passes down through you. Then imagine that this disc disappears off into the universe.

At that same point, at level 35 beneath you, a net ball made of the same microscopic diamond energy will begin to form, as you ask the CK energies to remove the debris, loosened by the first disc. Imagine the net ball forming around you and your aura, completely surrounding the outside of your energy field, and sealed at the top. You are now completely encased in a net ball of Crystal Ki diamond energy.

Then ask them to remove the debris and allow them to take the net slowly upwards through your aura, towards your feet and passing through your physical body, out through the top of your head and up through the aura above you, to level 35, much like a fishing trawler net. At this point have a look in your mind's eye to see what is in the net, then ask them take it to wherever God wills it to be, which is either into the Light, into the Central Flame, or back to where it came from. Then visualize it disappearing off into the universe, gone for good.

It is very important to fill the gaps and voids. (If you do not do this, you leave yourself wide open to be filled with more rubbish). Therefore imagine another disc forming just above the top of your aura at level 35 again and ask the CK energies to move the disc slowly down through your aura, your physical body and the aura beneath you to level 35. This disc will fill all of the gaps and voids with the perfect energy for you at this point of your journey. As diamonds contain all of the colours of the spectrum, your body will absorb the exact colour it needs. Crystal Ki energy also contains sound frequencies within the diamonds, so it is not unusual to hear sounds (if you are clairaudient) as it passes through you.

Sometimes the net may be too heavy to lift or have liquid in it. If this is the case, just ask for another net to be either water-tight or to be reinforced to make it stronger, and ask the CK energies to bring the new net ball around you, then through you and your aura again. You do not need to start the whole procedure again, just the netting part of it. Always remember, the Crystal Ki energies are there to help, and all you need to do is ask for guidance in your mind and you will receive it. Trust your intuition!

You can do this clearing on your house if you are sitting inside of it using the same procedure, but setting the intention to clear the house instead of, or as well as, you. If you want to use this technique on someone, and you are unable to seek their permission, you can ask permission from their higher self.

Asking permission of the higher self—The best way to do this is to sit quietly, take five or six deep breaths, then allow your breathing to find its own natural rhythm. Now invoke their higher self by saying, "I invoke the higher self of (INSERT THEIR NAME)." Say this three times, and when you have an image of them in your mind's eye, ask permission to carry out the energy clearing if it is for their highest good. If the response is anything other than a definite *"Yes,"* then <u>do not</u> perform the clearing, as you could be disrupting their karma, and that is not allowed, and it could have consequences for you. It is possible that the Universe is trying to teach them something, and you should allow that process to run its course.

The same is true with someone's property. Unless you have been given permission from the person who owns the property, you do not have any right to do an energy clearing on it, even if you detect any negative energy in there. You *are* allowed to clear the building you work in, but it is important to do it when the building is as empty as possible, and set the intention that you aim to only clear any negative energy contained within the building and not the people possibly still in there.

Remote or Distant Clearing

As with energy clearing, permission is always required to carry out remote healing on anyone.

Again, it is important that you are not going to be disturbed, as once you have started the procedure, you must see it through to completion, as not doing so can be counterproductive.

This involves the same technique except that you visualise the person you are intending to clear standing about 10m (33 feet) away from you. See them as transparent, in order to see the disc of light move through them easily. I visualise them standing in a sphere of energy surrounded by the universe, as my intention is to only help them with the clearing.

See the disc moving down from level 35 above them, through their aura and through their physical body, and out through the bottom of their feet into the aura below them. Visualise the net ball of light forming from below them at level 35 and around the sides of their aura and over the top of them to level 35 until they are completely surrounded in a sphere of CK diamond energy. Visualise the ball moving up through their aura, their physical body and the aura above them, collecting the debris and see it being taken away by the Crystal Ki energies.

Ask God and the energies to fill the voids with exactly what is needed and, again, wait a minute, visualising the second disc moving slowly down through them for this to happen before the clearing is complete.

To do this clearing on a building, the same procedure applies. Visualise the building as a simple glass box; this box represents the building you wish to cleanse. See the grid coming down from about 10m above the roof and down through the building, through each floor and then down into the ground about 10m below ground level will do.

Then, just as you would with a person, see the net ball of diamond energy surround the building and see it rising up from below the ground through the building and up into air 10m. At this point, I like to look to make sure that there is something in the net, before asking the Crystal Ki energies to take it to where God wills it to be. Then ask them to fill the gaps and voids and allow this to happen by visualising the second disc moving down through the building. It really is quite simple and effective, and practise is essential if you want your home or workplace to be clear.

If you have a problem seeing the net in your mind's eye, just imagine that it is happening, this is good enough, but just saying the words and not visualising it is pointless and it will not work.

Completed correctly, this procedure is very powerful and can be applied to people, animals, countries* and even Mother Earth* (*after completion of a Crystal Ki training course). I regularly clear the planet using this technique but could do with more like minds to learn the procedure, as working at this level takes a lot of energy. I find that I lose weight when I do a lot of planetary healing.

Tie Cutting

Tie-cutting is simple and can release us from unhealthy or controlling relationships, past traumas and much more. I have even used it to cut ties with my self-saboteur and asked the universe to bring in the improved version of me. Visualising that new me coming all of the way into my physical body and merging with my physical energy body, I'm sure, helped me to get motivated and to write this book.

Most people will have heard the old saying *"Tugging at my heart strings"*. These strings are real on an energetic level, albeit invisible to the naked eye. They are negative energetic psychic ties or connections. Tie-cutting literally cuts you free of these connections. People can drain your life force via these connections, leaving you feeling depleted when they have gone.

Not being able to move on from old lovers is the most common problem tie-cutting resolves, but many people need to cut ties with their own family as they can cause a lot of distress also. Using this visualisation technique will enable you to cut the ties to create freedom for you both.

1. First find a quiet place where you will not be disturbed and set your intention to cut only the negative ties with this other person.
2. Take 18 slow breaths …
   - breathe in through the nose, filling your whole body right down into the abdomen, and then breathe out through the mouth. Do this six times.
   - breathe in through the nose, filling the lungs and rib cage only, and breathe out through the mouth. Do this six times.
   - breathe in through the nose, just filling the upper chest this time and out through the mouth. Do this six times.
   - allow your breath to find its own natural rhythm.
3. Visualise the person standing about 10m away from you, and try to get a sense of the negative connection or tie. If you cannot see one don't worry, simply imagine a black ribbon connecting you both.
4. In your mind's eye imagine a pair of scissors cutting that ribbon and then say these words, and really mean them. This will release the energy between you both.

"I cut and release you with love and peace, I forgive you, I forgive me, I am totally free."

I have seen ropes, rods, chains and other things linking people together. Depending on what needs cutting, you can visualise using a sword for rope, bolt cutters for chains, scissors for ribbons or a laser for metal rods. Just visualising the tool coming in to the picture in your mind and cutting the negative tie will do the job.

5. Ask God to fill the gaps with whatever is necessary at this point in your journey and say thank you.

This technique can also be used to cut free earthbound spirits. I once had a client who had the spirit of her brother attached to her. She was now in her fifties but her brother had died when they were both children. During the treatment, her deceased brother told me that he wanted her to cut the cords that bound him to her, in order for him to pass over into the light. I did tell the lady and she was very grateful as she wanted her brother to be at peace. I took her into a meditative state and let her talk to her brother and say goodbye. It was very moving for all of us. She had had the chance to say goodbye to him.

I do love my work but sometimes it can get very emotional. I have been a medium and clairvoyant all of my life but I chose not to give readings as I found it too distressing to speak to people's relatives who had crossed over, but now I am happy to give soul readings to people, as I work directly with their soul and inform them of their life purpose, which is important. I use my clairvoyance to see inside people's physical and energetic bodies, also to see in the astral planes, gathering information to help my clients find solutions to ongoing issues and health problems.

Please note: negative ties with people as a result of fall-outs and disputes can be reconnected if you persist in arguing or bad-mouthing the person after you have cut ties with them. These connections can drain your energy and it is only yourself that you are hurting in the end. So my advice is to cut, release, and forgive once and for all.

It is okay to carry out tie-cutting with anyone around you as you have the right to be energetically free. This is not the same as energy clearing, which as I mentioned earlier, always requires permission.

Crystal Ki Healing Exercise

Important: this healing is not to be carried out without permission of the recipient or their Higher Self.

Please note that when speaking to the energies, you do not need to do it out loud, simply say it in your head, as they can hear your thoughts.

1. Prayer… *"Dear God, I ask that I am a channel of pure love and light, that all energies and information that comes to me, comes from you. I ask that this healing is for the highest good of all. Please bless and protect me as I work. Amen."*
2. Affirm… *"I call upon the Universal Crystal Ki Healing Energies and the Energies of Purification."* (3 times)
3. Affirm… *"My intention is to cut and release <u>only low frequency energies</u>, to clear all fear, pollution, symbols and low frequency ET's or entities. I ask Holy Spirit for a Crystal Ki disc and net, reinforced or watertight if necessary, to pass through my whole being and remove these energies."*
4. Take 18 slow breaths …
    - breathe in through the nose, filling your whole body right down into the abdomen, and then breathe out through the mouth. Do this six times.
    - breathe in through the nose, filling the lungs and rib cage only, and breathe out through the mouth. Do this six times.
    - breathe in through the nose, just filling the upper chest this time and out through the mouth. Do this six times.
    - allow your breath to find its own natural rhythm.

   This breathing technique stimulates the pineal gland and opens the mind's eye. It also helps you to relax.
5. Affirm… *"I ask the Crystal Ki Energies to bring the disc down through me now to clear imbalances as stated in my earlier intentions. **<u>If this be God's will, so be it, and so it is</u>**."* THIS IS VERY IMPORTANT!

6. Close your eyes, wait a minute, and *v*isualise a disc of Crystal Ki energy just above your aura at level 35, then slowly moving down from above your head and aura. Imagine it moving down slowly through your aura and physical body, then out of the soles of your feet through your aura again to level 35 below your aura. (You may feel a little lighter after this.)
7. Affirm.... *"I ask the Crystal Ki Energies to take these energies to be transformed and transmuted in the Central Flame, taken into the Light or be returned to where they came from, whichever is Gods will."*
8. Close your eyes and visualise a net ball of Crystal Ki diamond energy forming beneath your aura, starting at level 35 below you and surrounding your whole aura, all of the way up to level 35 above you and tied at the top. You and your aura are now surrounded in a net ball of Crystal Ki energy. Visualise the bottom of the ball moving upwards through the bottom of your aura, then slowly through your physical body and up into the air above you to level 35, collecting all of the debris that has been cut free. At this point you may have a look in your mind's eye to see or sense what is in it. Do not worry if you cannot sense anything, the clearing will still work. Then visualise the debris being taken away to where God wills it to be. (You may feel the energy change after this.)
9. Affirm ... ."*I ask Holy Spirit and the Crystal Ki Energies to please fill the voids with whatever is God's Will."* ... and visualise another disc passing down through you filling all of the gaps and voids with the perfect energy for you. **THIS IS VERY IMPORTANT!** Wait a minute while this takes place imagining the second disc passing down through you but slightly quicker than the first one.
10. Affirm... *"I ask my higher self to choose the protection and camouflage I may need at this moment in time on every layer of my aura."* Wait 10 or 20 seconds for that to settle in.

Thank God and the Crystal Ki Energies for helping you!!! Dismiss the angels with love and peace.

Please note: It is essential that you carry out this exercise as it is written and I advise you to use it with the utmost integrity, it is very powerful! If you are any doubt about using it, please contact info@thecrystalkifoundation.com for advice.

Check list

1. Prayer
2. Call in Angels
3. Set Intention
4. Breathing exercises
5. Ask for disc **(If it is God's will—Important)**
6. Visualise disc moving down
7. Ask for net and for debris to be taken to wherever is God's will
8. Visualise it moving up
9. Ask Holy Spirit for gaps and voids to be filled with whatever is God's will **(Very important!)**
10. Ask your higher self to surround you with protection and camouflage
11. Thank God and Angels

This technique can be used to remove all sorts of things such as toxins, negative belief patterns, and even the seed fear of enlightenment. The seed fear of enlightenment is a kind of etheric implant that we have placed in ourselves to block us from reaching the enlightenment level of consciousness. It relates back to when we were in Atlantis. We knew then that when we became enlightened we would, in effect, die and this is where the fear comes from. This fear can be removed easily and we now know that enlightenment does not mean sudden death, as there are many enlightened beings walking the planet, and hopefully there will be many more as we all work towards ascension.

I removed my seed fear as I found out it had been placed in me by myself in my previous life, having attained to the level of 904 on Dr Hawkins' Map of Consciousness. I became fearful of death and placed the block in my body as a result. The block looked like a huge sheet of steel, like a drain cover, splitting my body in two halves. It came out easily in the net but you do need to set the intention that you wish to remove the seed fear of enlightenment before you begin the procedure. Since I removed it, I feel much closer to Source.

Intention is important. Intention is the power behind the cleansing and, in fact, all healing work. With the help of the Universal Crystal Ki energies, you are changing etheric energy into spiritual energy when you condition it with spiritual intent. As a result, this energy will channel through your heart chakra and raise the frequency of the energy promoting a more positive result when performing healing, distant healing, global healing or enhancing meditation.

I never carry out any type of healing work without first setting clear intentions, and I would strongly advise you to do the same. These energies must be treated with respect. The intention makes the work happen in the correct manner. It is best to do this exercise when you are wide awake, as falling asleep half-way through would leave you wide open to all sorts of rubbish to make a nuisance of itself. I would also advise you to never work with energy when you have drugs or alcohol in your system, as this can be very dangerous.

28. Meditation and Brainwaves

Meditation is practised by many different people in all walks of life, for a wide variety of reasons. Some are religious, some spiritual, and some just for relaxation or stress management. Meditation is very helpful in allowing you to go within and helping you to forget about the worries of the world outside.

I would strongly recommend that you try to meditate on a daily basis, even if only for 5-10 minutes. It is a vital tool in order to ascend to higher realms of spirituality, and to access knowledge from a higher source. Meditation takes you into another state of consciousness and changes your brainwave frequency. There are four main states we can be in at any one time: Alpha, Beta, Delta and Theta, each having a different frequency measured in Hertz (Hz—cycles per second).

The dream state or very relaxed state is call the Alpha, and its frequency varies from between 8-13Hz. The normal active daily waking state is called the Beta state and is around 14-30Hz. When you are day-dreaming, meditating, shamanic journeying or similar, you are in the Theta state, which is between 4-7Hz. You are actually in this state when you are driving on the motorway and you can't remember the last few minutes of your journey. Scary stuff! The last state is Delta, and this is usually reached when you are in a deep sleep, usually around 3Hz or less.

I regularly practise meditation for spiritual reasons. I use it to connect to my higher self or Source, seeking divine wisdom. It is essential to my spiritual growth and has become a major part of my life. I certainly feel it if I miss my practise for a couple of days. Twenty minutes a day in deep meditation is usually all I need to find the answers to any problem I encounter. But I tend to meditate in my bath for an hour at a time. It also leaves me feeling very calm and relaxed, and mentally problem-free.

Problems are all relative to perception, and perception is illusory. Negative perceptions begin within the mind, and in order to eliminate the problem we need to ask God or Source to raise the frequency of our minds, and hence our perceptions. Infusing spiritual energy into the problem or situation raises the vibration and purifies the energy. This means that the problem is now either in a higher frequency range or has even been resolved instantaneously, due to the effect of higher consciousness and the change in perception.

For example, a while ago, I had arrived at Birmingham airport after an eight hour overnight flight. I was exhausted as I did not sleep, and I had ordered a taxi to be waiting for me when I arrived, so as to get home as soon as possible. Needless to say, the cab did not turn up. I was angry at first, but then remembered that I could change my reality by asking for Divine help. I asked God to help me get home, and two minutes later a taxi driver who was waiting for his pre-booked fare came over and asked if I was going to Warwick University. I said no but I wanted to get home to Warwick and my cab had let me down. His fare had let him down too, so we were the answer to both of our problems. My solution had come immediately I asked God to help. It really does work. Just believe and give it a try.

Practising meditation helps to clear the mind of problems and clutter, and is fairly easy to learn. The following breathing technique can be used to reach the Theta state of brainwaves. It stimulates the pineal gland, opening the astral doorway to other levels of consciousness and dimensions. I also use it to bring my clients into a semi-meditative state and to help them to relax at the beginning of a session.

You will need to find a quiet place where you will not be disturbed. I always visualise a protective sphere of light around me, and state that I am safe and protected by the Universe before I begin.

Either sit with your back straight, or lie down with a small pillow under your head. Set an alarm clock for 10-20 minutes in case you fall asleep. Before you start, you can set a subject for your meditation to be based on, or you can ask a question of your higher self or Source.

Close your eyes and take six long, slow deep breaths in through your nose and filling your whole body with air, allowing your chest and stomach to rise and right down into your abdomen then slowly breathe out through your mouth. With each of the six breaths feel yourself relaxing more and more and visualise any stress leaving your body in the out breath.

Take six slow breaths into your lungs only, expanding the chest, breathing in through the nose and out through the mouth.

Take six slow breaths into the upper chest only, once again in through the nose and out through the mouth.

Allow your breath to find its own natural rhythm and just relax for a couple of minutes. Relax and let the information you need come into your mind, and feel the peace flow through your whole body.

When your alarm goes off, slowly bring your attention back into the room and drink some water to ground yourself.

If you still feel a bit light-headed, visualise a sphere of light around your Earth Star chakra, approximately 30cm (12 inches) below the soles of you feet—see diagram 1 above. Intend for the outside of the sphere to be camouflaged, if you feel the need. I always do this as it makes it more difficult for lower frequency energies to be able to see you. Set the intention that the sphere is to act as a protective filter and to purify any energy coming into your body via the chakras on the soles of your feet.

Then take your attention to the top of your head (Crown chakra) and visualise a line of light moving down from your Crown, through your main channel along the front of the spine, down your legs and out of your feet into your Earth Star chakra inside the sphere in the ground below your feet. You have now grounded your energy by doing this, and should feel less light-headed.

There are many types of meditation technique. Here are three examples:

Mindfulness meditation
Open focus; remaining in the here and now; shifting from one thought to the next with ease; complete acceptance of all things. The person constantly brings the mind back to the now and does not analyse or fantasise in any way.

Concentrated Meditation
This is about being focused on an object or repeating a mantra or prayer.

Buddhist Meditation
This includes Shamantha, which is focused on a single subject, and Vipassana, which is aimed at developing wisdom and insight through seeing the truth.

There are many other types of meditation and I advise you to read about a few before choosing one. Some methods involve keeping the eyes open and staring at a particular point or object. I found this difficult and it made my eyes water. When I meditate, I ask Archangel Michael to be my guide (mentor) and I just wait for my higher self or Source to deliver any information I may need.

I would advise you to have a mentor present when you meditate or journey, as they can give you help and advice. A mentor can be a Saint, your

Guardian Angel or even your deceased Grandma. It does not matter who you choose. Just asking them in your mind is enough; saying their name three times will bring them into the scenario.

Sometimes I journey to wherever my soul wishes me to go, or I consciously ask to be taken to a specific place. This could be anywhere from the top of a mountain to inside my own body. I would not advise you to try to journey without having had some teaching, or asking for a spirit to guide and teach you. Journeying takes practise and care but once you become adept, there are no limits to inter-dimensional travel.

When I first started to meditate, I found it difficult; then I began to see coloured clouds of light and then an eye that, eventually, winked at me. Seeing an eye is quite common. Apparently an open eye represents a higher level of consciousness than a closed one. Now I travel to the most amazing places and go inside my own body to balance any disharmony I find, using visualisation and the power of the mind. This is often referred to as psychic surgery.

It is important to drink a glass of water after you have been meditating, as it will help to ground you. Over 75% of our body is water and as we raise our vibration, it is important that we drink more of it. Eight glasses a day are recommended; it may sound like a lot but it is so important. As your body is becoming less dense and as you become lighter, the water helps you to hold more light.

Meditation Practices

Having found a quiet place, connected to your higher self, asked your mentor to be your guide, and completed the breathing exercises described above, you then enter the meditative state. Now you can choose a subject for your meditation.

In order to gain insight into any illness and disharmony in the body, for example, the following is helpful to find out exactly what is causing the problem and what you need to do in order to heal yourself. Once in the meditative state of consciousness, you are now ready to talk to the different layers of your body, namely the physical, emotional, mental and spiritual; then for greater insight, your higher self. Remember, we consist of various energetic layers, each one having a consciousness of its own, and each one needing attention in order for us to be healthy and balanced individuals.

Set the intention that you wish to gain insight into the particular illness or imbalance, and be specific with your intent. These are my two favourite questions:

"What do you need from me to correct the imbalance in my body" and
"Do you have a message for me?"

Now visualise a bright corridor with five doors, two on the left, two on the right and one at the end. When I say visualise, I do not mean you have to see amazing visions. The images can be similar to when you are dreaming. Imagining the corridor will work just as well. Some people see their bodies as people, others just feel a presence, and both are fine. The information is the important thing, not the picture.

Walk towards the first door on your left, this is where your physical self resides. Go into the room and ask your physical self the two questions above. You can ask more, but try not to ask too many, as you will take ages to get to the other end of the corridor. Wait for the reply. Because you are in an altered state of consciousness, the answer will just come into your mind. Trust this process.

It is very common for the answer to be *"I need love"*. At this point you can tell your physical self that you love it and give it a hug, if necessary. You can do this in your mind by visualising it happening. Remember that all communication is telepathic when you are meditating. Thank it for the information and leave the room.

Move on to the first door on the right of the corridor; this is your emotional self. Ask the same questions and receive the answers. Give thanks and move on.

Through the second door on the left is where your mental self resides. Ask the same questions, receive the answers, and having given thanks, move on.

The next room on the right contains your spiritual self. Ask the questions and when you have received your answers and given thanks, again, move on.

The final door at the end of the corridor is where your higher self resides. Enter the room, ask your questions and, as before, give thanks. Leave the room and walk back to the other end of the corridor, bringing yourself slowly back into the room where you are sitting. Drink some water to ground yourself.

Now you have the information needed, hopefully to correct the imbalance in your body. I did this to gain insight into how to balance my physical body when I was ill, and the results of the meditation taught me how to resolve the problem.

Once you become more adept at this technique you will not need to do the full meditation and you can help other people gain insight about their illness or use it to help clients.

For example, if you want to find out how to help a family member who is ill, you can communicate through meditation and your higher self, connecting with their physical, emotional, mental, spiritual and higher self in order to gain insight in to how to help them become balanced. Use your breathing technique to take you into a higher state of consciousness, as with the meditation. Then simply ask your higher self to communicate with their higher self. Then ask each individual body what it needs, as you did before. You do not need to go through the corridor meditation, just ask one at a time and visualise that body in your mind's eye. Remember to give thanks and move on to the next, until you have the information you need. Eventually, as you raise your vibration, you will be able to communicate with ease and no longer need the long breathing technique to connect to your higher self, as it will be almost instantaneous.

If it is not karmic or genetic, disease in the physical is usually caused by an imbalance in one or more of the other bodies, and this technique can be very helpful in contacting other parts of the human psyche, such as the inner child. We can find out what the problem is and take the action needed to correct the imbalance on many levels.

Crystal Skull Meditation

One of the favourite meditations I had involved a crystal skull. During the meditation I could see a quartz crystal skull coming down from above my head and merging with my own skull. It felt positive and I knew I was safe. Once in position, a tube of light projected from the bottom of the skull and moved downwards, filling my whole spine with a brilliant light. A ball of it collected at my heart centre and rays of light, hundreds of them, radiated out, moving around just like a laser show.

This continued for a few minutes and then stopped. I was unsure what was happening exactly, but had a strong feeling of being given information that I would use at a later date. The skull disappeared as quickly as it had arrived. I felt as if something had encoded my DNA. I had no idea what that information might be, however I was convinced that I had been energetically rewired, with gold wires covered in a white sheath permeating my whole body, with hundreds of wires running through me just like fibre optics. It felt as if I had received a completely new nervous system.

Shortly after this I could see an image of the Sphinx and a stairway leading down to an inside room. What appeared to be a throne made of a 4ft diameter tree was in front of me, and I felt the need to sit on the tree. Immediately a bright tube of light surrounded me and a large leather-bound book appeared on my lap. The book opened from back to front, turning page by page, all of its own accord. I just held it. Then the book opened again, and began to flick in the opposite direction, and as it did so, each page began to fill with writing. Once the book was full, the tube of light disappeared and I walked out of the room and made my way home.

I had read about the 'Mystery of the Crystal Skulls' when I was in Sri Lanka and was convinced that the skull that came to me was to do with that, and that the information in it was to do with this book.

According to Native American legends, there are thirteen crystal skulls that exist on Earth, some with movable jaws, which have the ability to heal, sing and speak. Apparently they contain spiritual entities with important information about the destiny of mankind, and other answers to the great mysteries of life.

One legend says that there are twelve planets in the cosmos inhabited by human beings, and that there is one skull for each of these planets, and one further skull, which is vital to the whole.

These skulls are in various locations, some still hidden and kept safe by their keepers, some privately owned, and others housed in museums all over the world.

According to legend, it is said that one day, when mankind is more evolved and pure enough to use the skulls for the highest good of all, the skulls will be brought together and they will share their great wisdom with mankind. I look forward to that day.

29. Ancestral Healing

We are all linked to our ancestors, and taking healing back through them can have excellent results for your healing process. It is amazing what you can inherit. Depending on the disease, ancestral healing can also help with genetic illness.

You can invoke your ancestors to work with you. At a spiritual level, time and space impose no restrictions, so in one sense, your ancestors are living concurrently with you. Be guided by their knowledge and wisdom.

This type of healing should be done slowly, and in a meditative state, in the same way as a journey session would be carried out. You can tune into a specific illness and from whom it originated. You can carry out distant healing as you would on a person sitting in front of you. You may need to do several treatments, seeking to balance emotional, mental, spiritual, as well as physical energies. When you have completed the healing, sense or visualise it coming back through the ancestral ladder to you, and, if you have them, to your children. You can repeat this until you feel you have balanced the energies in all of your main ancestors. As soon as you free yourself of a block, you free your children and grandchildren too.

It is possible for us to send healing backward and forward seven generations or more with intention and visualisation. Simply call in the Crystal Ki healing energies as usual, setting the intention with them that you would like to send healing back seven generations and forward seven generations through all of your direct ancestors. Remember that these energies can travel to the past and the future instantly; they are not restricted by time and space, so it is easy for them to do this.

I like to visualise myself with a separate sphere of light in front of each of my main chakras, each with its own wings, and set the intention that each sphere will cleanse as it moves through its chakra. I then visualise the sphere fly through me and through a line of seven people, symbolising my ancestors, standing behind me (representing the past), and then I see it come back the same way, clearing the chakras as it moves through each person.

I then see seven people in front of me and do the same thing again, seeing the sphere of light move forward through them, clearing the chakras as it goes and bringing the sphere back through to me. Remember to set the intention of the healing before you start. You can ask to heal specific problems or even karmic issues. I then send another sphere through every chakra, but this time I set an intention to fill each chakra with healing energy and to fill any gaps.

You can bring this grid of light through your ancestors once you become adept at the tie-cutting and space clearing process. I visualise stacking the seven ancestors inside one another like Russian dolls, and perform a distant clearing on them. You may find another visualisation that works well for you.

30. Animal Medicines

According to Shamanic teachings it is possible to pull in the energetic powers of certain animals in order to gain their strengths and abilities. I have used the following simple technique of connecting with the animal kingdom for years, and it has been very beneficial. All you need to do is to invoke the energy/medicine of a particular animal, and that is done by simply saying the following:

"I invoke the energy of the (insert the name of the animal here)" (Repeat 3 times).

Insert the name of the animal you require to help or guide you and always remember to thank it for its help. Animals are telepathic too, just like angels, so you can say it in your head and not out loud. The following animals are my favourite, and you will find many others if you research shamanic animal medicine on the internet:

Dolphin	Healing and wisdom
Dog	Loyalty and nurturing abilities
Unicorn	Enlightenment
Salmon	Strength when life feels like an uphill struggle
Duck	Nurturing abilities
Geese	Connection with Soul groups
Tiger	Seize opportunities as they arise
Spiders	Creativity
Pigeons and Doves	Monogamy and love
Butterfly	Transformation
Badger	Defending one's territory when needed
Sea Horse	Purity of Mind, Perfection

Tree Medicines

In a similar way, we can also gain healing and wisdom by connecting with the tree medicines, by invoking their essence with the intention to heal, or meditating with them in mind. You can invoke the essence of a particular tree by simply saying the following and inserting the name of the tree you would like to help you:

"I invoke the essence of the (insert the name of the tree here) tree" (Repeat 3 times).

Here are a few examples of tree healing qualities:

Holly
On an energetic level Holly helps to soften our 'prickly' edges. Meditating with Holly can help us to gain wisdom and the ability to make better choices. It is a popular Bach flower remedy used to alleviate anger; it is good for calming oversensitive people and also hatred or aggression. Folklore tells us that Holly leaves and berries can cure smallpox, help mend broken bones. It is also considered a lucky charm.

Pine (Scotch)
Distillation of the Scotch pine needles allows a beautiful essential oil to be produced. The aromatic properties of Scotch pine essential oil include decongestant, analgesic, expectorant, deodorant and anti-inflammatory. The oil can be used to warm the hands and feet and it also improves the body's resistance to germs.

Hazel
Hazel is probably best known for the medicinal uses of Witch-hazel, made from the leaves of the North American tree. This produces an astringent, which is a chemical compound used to constrict or shrink body tissue. Witch-hazel is mainly used on bruises, swelling and sores. It is also used to help skin problems and acne.

Silver Birch
When the oil is distilled from the leaves, Silver Birch has many medicinal uses such as treating psoriasis and eczema. The leaves are used to reduce swelling and to alleviate fluid retention. The sap is a mild diuretic. The bark can be used as a lotion to help clear acne and more serious skin problems.

Apple
Apple trees are members of the Rose family. The pectin's found in apples are a good regulator for the digestive system and bowel movements. Apple juice is said to stimulate the production of saliva and an apple before bed is said to aid sleep as it has mild sedative qualities.

Oak
Oak tree essence gives us strength and the energy to achieve our goals. The mighty Oak has antiseptic and anti-inflammatory properties and is used to aid tooth and gum care. Oak tree bark is brewed into a tea and drunk to aid the healing of varicose veins, haemorrhoids, and to reduce fevers.

Elm
Elm is used to aid purification: slippery elm works effectively to remedy many digestive ailments such as irritable bowel syndrome, haemorrhoids, diarrhoea, colitis, ulcers and heartburn. Elm remedy is said to be good for those who feel overwhelmed. Apparently, the inner bark can be ground up and made into a porridge which is highly nutritious and is full of antioxidants, with a similar consistency and taste to oatmeal.

Rowan
In folklore, some say that if you plant Rowan in your front garden, it will keep witches away from your door. The fruits of the Rowan are made into Jams, Juices and jellies, the berries must be cooked first of course. Rowan fruit contain Vitamin C and the berries can be used to regulate the digestion because it helps against diarrhoea and constipation.

Willow
This is my favourite tree. It is believed that the ancients used the leaves and bark of the beautiful tree as a remedy for aches and fevers. Willows contain salicin, a substance that chemically resembles aspirin and is said

to temporarily relieve stomach ache, headache and other pains. The willow branch is one of the chief attributes of Kwan Yin, the bodhisattva of compassion. Willows flower essence promotes forgiveness, acceptance of what is and taking responsibility for one's life situation.

Note: The above is for information only and not meant to be used as medicinal guidance, please seek the advice of a medical professional if you choose to use any of the remedies or medicines mentioned in this chapter.

31. Akashic Records: Breaking Vows, Pacts, Contracts or Agreements

It is more than likely that we will all have made some sort of vow, pact, bond, contract or agreement in previous lives. If these are still in place, these contracts can have serious repercussions in this life, where they may no longer be appropriate. For example, if at some time in the past, you made a vow of celibacy, it could affect your sex life today. Vowing to take revenge on old enemies could mean you are energetically tied to someone in this life, and that connection could be draining your energy. It could mean you are tied to a group of people who are bad for you, but you find it hard to break away from them.

Tie-cutting and breaking old vows will resolve the problem. This exercise is very useful, as it terminates these vows, pacts, bonds, contracts and agreements for good. I would recommend finding a quiet place and taking some deep breaths, as you would before performing the tie-cutting exercise, and then affirm the following:

Affirm ... *"I call upon the presence and assistance of the Crystal Ki Energies of Purification and I offer this healing for Mother Earth and all sentient beings everywhere."* (Say this once)

Repeat the words *"Akashic Records"* (Say this 3 times).

Affirm... *"In the name of God, the First Source and Centre, I command that all negative vows, pacts, bonds, contracts and agreements, past, present and future, known and unknown, not for the highest good between me and...INSERT FULL*

NAME OF PERSON… are brought here now and burned and transmuted by the central flame, registered null and void." (Say this 3 times)

Close your eyes and imagine a well in front of you with a furnace at the bottom and a huge library beyond that.

Affirm… *"I ask the Crystal Ki Energies to take the vows, pacts, bonds, contracts and agreements to be burned and transmuted in the Central Flame. If this is God's will, so be it and so it is!"* (Say this once)

Visualise this taking place until you feel they are all burned, and ask the angels to let you know when they are finished. It is vital that you visualise or imagine the vows, etc, being burned. Simply saying it is not enough.

Important: Ask God and the angels to fill the voids with whatever is needed at this moment in time.

Thank God and the Crystal Ki Energies for helping you!

By changing the intention and wording at the beginning of the exercise, this process can also be used to void curses, hexes, spells, voodoo and black magic.

32. Journey Work

My son came home from school one day and said that two teachers had been following him around all day, *"That's strange,"* I thought, and then it dawned on me that the magic mirror was trying to tell me something.

The next morning during my meditation and clearing session I could see in my mind's eye two Red Indian chiefs sitting in my lounge. They looked harmless enough, but I did a space clearing and pulled a net through the room and they both passed straight through it, so I felt sure that they were for my highest good. They both looked very impressive, with lots of feathers around their headbands. I felt quite honoured. One was in his mid thirties and the other one looked about sixty.

I soon realised that these were the two teachers my son had mentioned, and that they had been following me around trying to get my attention. In the end, they stayed for months and taught me how to journey through the other realms and what to look out for, the good and the bad; they told me about shape-shifting, and the Trickster.

Tricksters can take many forms and shapes. According to Native American folklore, the Trickster can take the form of any creature or messenger; he is the Fool and can appear in different shapes that could either be human or animal. Some stories have the Trickster as a raven or a coyote. Tricksters will either do you good or be harmful, leading you down the wrong path just for fun, so it is important to trust your gut instinct or intuition when journeying. If it feels suspect, it usually is. When I journey, if something I encounter feels suspect, I ask Archangel Michael (my mentor) to catch it in a Crystal Ki net and remove it from my path. Generally if the net passes through it, then I know it presents no threat to me.

My new guides called me Lone Tree and worked with me for a long time until I was adept at journeying. I was tested at various times, failed sometimes, but passed more than not, and felt secure with my new-found skills.

When you journey inter-dimensionally, the world is your oyster, and you can travel to magical, mystical places, meeting all kinds of fascinating creatures. You can become as small as a flea, or hold the whole planet in your hand. There are no limits, and because of the diversity of this practice I have journeyed often, and learnt many things.

I journey my clients and take them to a wide variety of places. Some may need to go into a secret garden to meet another soul who will talk to them and give them advice; others may journey inside their own body to help find out what is causing an imbalance, and find a healing solution. Some of these sessions are very 'Dr Who' and great fun. I am a guide and help my clients find what they need but their inner wisdom is in control of where they travel to, and what they find when they get there.

33. Crystal Ki Healing—Case Studies and Soul Retrieval

Sarah

Sarah was 39 years old and recovering from cancer of the cervix. Sarah was very down and during her first treatment with me, I noticed black serpent-type energy in her sacral and promptly removed it using a net of light. It hissed at me when I pulled it out of her chakra!

I generally perform a tie-cutting at the start of treatments, and on the second treatment with Sarah I began to notice a spirit around her that was not for her highest good. When I journeyed her she could see a man, he looked quite dark to me, and I did a tie-cutting to remove him. Sarah did not find him a threat but I was not sure about him at all. There was also a tall, gold, light-being with her, who looked to be extra-terrestrial. He was very light and obviously a good soul who appeared every time she came to see me. He must have been one of her guides; he had a calm presence about him.

On Sarah's third treatment we decided that we should perform a soul retrieval. I explained to her what this meant and advised her that the process could not be rushed. I explained that it would be vital to her healing process to work towards finding the soul fragmentation: this is the part of our essence or subconscious, in her case her inner child, that has been lost or locked itself away due to some kind of trauma or upset. It is vital that when you find the lost soul fragment, you ask it what it needs and meet its request, before it can be integrated back into the heart of the client. This lost soul fragment can be an adult part of us, but in my experience, I have found that the people I deal with usually have a small child that needs to be returned. The aim is to integrate that child essence back into the heart chakra of the client, allowing them to let go of the past, and to feel whole again. It is a process that can have profound effects.

Sarah continued to come to me, and on the fifth treatment I recommended that she took some flower essence remedies to help aid her with the recovery, and to release old energy from the system. By the sixth treatment she looked bright and happy when she arrived. However she had been reading about cancer and the causes of it, as she had wanted to know why she had contracted cancer in the first place, I tried to explain that it was linked to her childhood, but she needed confirmation, so before we journeyed, we set the intention that the answer was to be found today. She eventually saw her younger self, hiding in a wardrobe.

I explained that we would be able to speak using telepathy to this part of her psyche, and that we needed to integrate the frightened child back into her heart chakra in order to return this soul fragment to where it was meant to be. We had difficulty in reassuring the child that she would be loved and would be safe if she came back into adult Sarah's heart. I explained that she would be safe and that Sarah's heart was full of love and a beautiful place to be. The whole process was quite strange for Sarah and she was amazed that when she asked the little girl if she could hear me she said *"Yes,"* even though all communication at soul level was done telepathically. I would speak to adult Sarah but use telepathy to communicate with her inner child.

Within ten minutes the child Sarah was back home within adult Sarah's heart, right where she belonged, and I could see her dancing and skipping in my mind's eye as I poured more love energy into Sarah's heart chakra.

Little Sarah only looked around five years old, with her hair plaited, and wearing a pretty dress with baby doll shoes, she held a toy doll in her hands. I explained this to adult Sarah and praised child Sarah for helping big Sarah to grow and healing her. The little girl even blew me a kiss.

Sarah was still unclear as to what caused her cancer and I took it upon myself to ask why, as a child, she would hide in a wardrobe. She said it was because her mother would say that she was going to put her into a home. We had already cut ties with her mum, which had helped with the healing process. Threatening a child like that can be traumatic enough to trigger one bad cell memory; that cell can lay dormant for years but then turn cancerous, in this case, later in life. The whole process of finding your soul and forgiving all concerned is important in order to release the root cause of the disease. The cancer formed in her emotional chakra, which made sense. Sarah needed to go home and assimilate the whole thing. I warned that she might feel emotional for a week or two as the returned soul fragment settled in. It was also important to feed the newly integrated child with some childish fun to make her feel at home.

Kim

Kim's mother had advised her to book an appointment with me. When she arrived Kim was very low and had a victim consciousness (e.g. *"Why me, I always get the bad luck"*). Kim was only in her thirties but was in a bad way, and in the first visit I felt the need to do a Tie Cutting from her ex-boyfriend, in order to energetically free her from him. I explained about victim consciousness and that negative thinking only created more negativity. She was a bright woman and seemed to understand and grasp what I was saying immediately. Kim was one of those people you can easily take a shine too. She was a likable soul.

I balanced her head and heart chakras; her head was full of negative thought forms, entities and belief systems and it took me some time to clear it, but I knew she was going to need more treatments and, after talking to her at the initial consultation, a soul retrieval very quickly. I needed to get her into a better mindset, and I made sure she understood that positive attracts positive and negative attracts negative. I spent extra time talking to her and teaching her about how we create our lives with our thoughts and feelings. She grasped the advice and put it into practise; she bought the movie 'The Secret' and soon began to fly.

The change was amazing; after only two treatments she was smiling and confident, even optimistic. By the third visit she had met a new man, a good man, but her old way of victim thinking was starting to creep back in, so we decided she needed to do a tie-cutting with that part of herself, namely her self-saboteur. Kim was shocked when she saw her darker self in the visualisation; we cut ties with her, asking the Universe to send her the new, happy version. She could see the new her walking towards her, hugging her and absorbing the new her into her body; with that, we had brought in the shining positive Kim, and integrated her new essence.

Kim went on to start telling others about positive thinking after only two or three treatments herself. She was a quick learner and I enjoyed working with her. By the fourth treatment she was happy, still with her new man, and really positive in her attitude.

Kim told me how her stepmother would lock her in a cupboard in the dark when she was little, and it became clear why she had problems with men, as she blamed her father, as he was not around when this was going on. Men treated Kim badly because she had victim mentality. If you see yourself as a victim the Universe will send you people who will abuse you and treat you badly. You create your abuser! Only you can change your situation by changing your negative thinking and belief systems.

Kim told me that she hated her stepmother and I explained that hate is so powerful that it will keep her attached to this woman in this and the next life, or until she forgives her. I asked her, even if she could not forgive the personality to forgive the soul, with the soul being the pure part of her essence, and with that in mind, I took Kim through the process of cutting the ties, and she cut them with ease.

However, the strangest thing happened at the beginning of Kim's journey, when she was walking through a wood, and she saw a woman keep popping her head out from behind the trees. I told her that the woman (her stepmother) wanted to help her find her soul fragment and help her to heal and repair the damage. Kim accepted this and she agreed to hold hands with this woman—to my amazement as only ten minutes ago, Kim had said that she hated her. They both went into a small house in the woods where the child Kim was waiting, sitting on the floor.

Kim's inner child would not talk or look the adult Kim in the eye. She would not hug her and was angry with adult Kim. She was very unhappy. I decided to do a tie-cutting and clear the energy between them. This helped and the child Kim decided to reunite if adult Kim would promise her safety and love, which adult Kim did, and the child Kim jumped back into the heart chakra in a flash. This was a fairly straightforward soul retrieval.

About a month later I heard more about Kim, when a friend of mine who knew Kim's family said that they had seen a great improvement in such a short period of time. She was much happier and optimistic and no longer had the victim mentality, which I was pleased to hear. Kim was so impressed with her treatments that she decided to do two workshops with me. She now has a much brighter outlook on life.

During one treatment she was having with me, she was shown her past and her future and in her future she could see herself in a lovely home, happily married with a man she truly loved, and with another child, a vision which made her very happy.

Alexandria

Alexandria was a young woman who was due to have a hernia operation three weeks after her first treatment with me. She believed in angels and they were very involved in the healing we carried out. There were lots of old emotional problems linked to the sacral chakra and they seemed to be the cause of the hernia. This woman had also been sexually abused as a young girl and this had left her feeling guilty and angry.

Once we cleared these emotions, we got to work on repairing the area inside her abdomen, and I held my hands there for at least thirty minutes or more before feeling the area was more stable. She said she was very aware of movement inside her body as this was happening.

I was told by my higher consciousness that she needed one more treatment in three weeks time, and then she was to allow the body another three weeks to heal before making a decision about having the operation.

I told her this and she said she would postpone her operation for one month and we agreed to meet three weeks later. The following month I carried out another treatment in which we looked at the inner child issues and healed them, then worked with repairing the damage in the abdomen using my hands on her body holding that area.
She called me a few weeks later to say she had been to the doctors and there was no sign of the hernia. Her husband didn't believe it and she was

referred to another doctor but again the results came back clear. It had worked, and we were both really pleased!

This particular woman had almost been killed in a car crash and had had many illnesses and operations in her lifetime—too many! During the treatment, we discovered that, during a bout of depression, she had made a death wish. We were told that this intention had been the cause of the car crash and many of her other problems. I decided to take her into the Akashic records to remove and cancel the death wish in the hope that her life would improve as a result, and so far so good.

If only people realised that words are powerful and they do have an effect on our lives for many years, especially wishes, oaths and the like. If you have made any kind of death wish, it can be cancelled by using the techniques in Shapter 31 on the Akashic records.

Everything in the physical world has a frequency or vibration; the lower vibrations being more solid and hence physical, and the higher being more pure and spiritual. Long-term negative emotional states of mind, such as being frightened, envious, judgemental, angry, unforgiving, or worried, create low frequency vibrations, and low frequency diseases can manifest as a result. The frequency of cancer, for example, is not compatible with the physical body, and it will devour the cells accordingly. Clearly, negative feelings can have a direct and damaging effect on someone's health.

Your whole life can be affected by a negative mind-set and energy, and because how you feel inside is reflected back into your reality, your perception will be that life is full of problems. Not only can this damage your health but your relationships and your career as well.

The trick is to recognise this negative mental attitude, then to take action to put it right by taking responsibility for your mind and your thoughts. Try to stop seeing yourself as a victim of life and set the intention to see yourself as getting better every day. Then act upon that intention, starting with positive thinking and a better diet, as good food has a massive effect on our mental health. Let go of any guilt, as that is self-destructive, and work towards raising your frequency in the physical, emotional, mental and spiritual levels. Happiness and balance will change things rapidly.

Beth

Beth was another girl in her thirties who came to me needing a soul retrieval, and we came across the lost part of her soul in a different way than was usual. Generally I would come across a key in the journey process, and that would unlock a cage or box to find the soul fragment. There was no key or a cage or anything like that for Beth. This lost part of her, the young girl, just walked up to her when she was on a beach in the meditation that we were doing as part of the treatment. Beth could see this young girl walking towards her and realised it was herself when she was nine years old.

This was different to previous experiences, and when this young girl was asked what it was she needed she insisted that the now older Beth had a dance with her on the beach, which older Beth found very strange. She danced in the sand, just as the young girl wanted, as older Beth needed to let her inner child play, and have fun, to lighten up, laugh and reconnect with the child-like side of her nature. She visualised this happening, and danced and sang with the younger version of herself and in no time at all she embraced that child, and that part of her was then integrated into her heart chakra with great ease. This was simple soul retrieval.

Mary

I have also worked with re-birthing and an example of this was experienced with a woman who was 30 years old. Mary had issues with moving forward in her life and felt something was blocking her. This was causing her anxiety problems, because of her lack of direction. A few people had mentioned to her that she could possibly benefit by going through a re-birthing process. I offered her my assistance and gave her some background on my experience and knowledge. Due to the fact that she was so anxious I visited her at home and began to work with her.

Starting with the breathing techniques that I use to get people into a semi-meditative state of consciousness, I then visually took Mary down in a lift and into the womb, where she stayed for a few minutes. I asked if she was alright and Mary said that she felt a little nervous and wanted someone with her. We decided to call on the soul of her sister to whom she was very close. They were best friends. Being inside the womb, with her sister holding her hand, she felt much more stable and happier to move forward. When Mary was ready I asked her to visualise a doorway and asked her to walk through it. Beyond the door was a long curvy tube, much like you would imagine the birth canal would be. When she got to the end there was another doorway and beyond that a beautiful room with a big bed and couch; the whole room was yellow and gold.

Once in the room, I asked her if she needed anything and she said she wanted to go and lie down. I let her relax and rest for a while. Again, when she was ready, I guided Mary's awareness back into the bedroom and it was over; the re-birthing was complete.

From what I have been told, she is happy and getting on with her life. Apparently she is now learning about angel therapies and crystal therapies and is quite enlightened in that respect.

34. Soul Purpose

When we get older, many of us will look back and see what we have achieved, or in some cases, what we haven't. It is important to put something into this world, and we all have a purpose, with each soul having its own personal mission. It may be simply to learn gratitude and forgiveness, or to become a spiritual teacher or even a world leader. I believe my purpose is to be a teacher, teaching about healing, self-purification and spiritual growth, and this book is an important part of that purpose. The tie-cutting and energy clearing is very special and powerful information, and this was the best way to get it out into the world.

Movies and books like *'The Secret'* inform us about the laws of attraction and teach us to have gratitude for the many blessings we have in our lives, but if your goal is significantly different from the plan your soul had for you before you were born, then you are less likely to achieve it. In that situation, it is important for you to find out what your soul purpose is, and to take steps towards setting goals that are more achievable.

Many people believe that your soul is the self-aware essence of your being, and is the true basis of your wisdom. Your soul is immortal and therefore existed prior to each incarnation and lifetime. With each life you will have a new agenda, based on your soul's growth from previous incarnations. We are all here to learn and grow, some with more active roles than others, whereas some just go along with their job and their home life without really questioning. If asked if they were happy, they might say *"Yes, my life is okay,"* but is that really enough? Do you really just want an okay life? If it could be better would you change it? Or would you carry on and ignore your heart's desires? There is no need to strive to be a world leader if you don't want to, but at least aim for something that makes you happy, something that makes your heart sing.

We are not here to just survive, and discovering our true purpose is important, because when we live our truth we evolve; life has more meaning, we become more creative and we live with a higher level of awareness and integrity.

If you find out that your soul purpose is very important and you find the thought of it overwhelming, don't worry. The Universe arranges it so that there are three souls incarnate and assigned to each important purpose, so if you do not want to go ahead with your specific soul purpose, there is someone else who will. The job will get done, and you do not need to feel guilty because you changed your mind. The Universe is in control of all eventualities, so worry not.

There are many books and CDs on the market that can help you to decide what your purpose is, and if you choose to discover more, you may find yourself embarking on a journey that will be transformative and empowering.

Many years ago, I was told by a woman that I was a medium and a clairvoyant. I was also told that I would be involved in public speaking. At the time I was sceptical and did not take a lot of notice, but a little later I found myself speaking at the Leamington Spa Peace Festival to thousands of people. I was terrified but I faced my fear and took the microphone and stood on the bandstand and spoke about peace and self-healing. The words seemed to channel through me from another source, and it just flowed. The woman was right and I have spoken to other groups since then, and I really enjoy it. Because of this experience I now believe that public speaking is also an important part of my purpose, and look forward to talking to more audiences in the near future.

35. 3rd Dimensional Signs

When I began to work with angels and spirit guides, there was always a part of my logical mind that questioned the guidance I was getting, or put what I received down to an over-active imagination. The logical (left) side of my brain was well developed; maths and science came easily to me, my job as a draughtsperson proved that. The intuitive and creative (right) side of my brain, the more feminine aspect, needed to be further developed, and as a result, initially, I did not feel comfortable trusting my intuition.

I had begun to develop many of the psychic senses, such as clairvoyance, which means vision using the mind's eye, and also images and messages in the physical world, the 3rd dimension. I began to get clairsentience, which means feeling people's emotions. Claircognisance enables you to receive messages in the forms of thoughts directly into the mind. Clairaudience means receiving guidance in the form of verbal messages either in your mind or with your ears directly from spirit, and clairomniscience, which relates to instant knowingness.

With all of these senses blossoming, my life began to get busy very quickly, and I was still finding my feet and a little apprehensive until someone prompted me to ask my guides to use another form of communication— what a brilliant idea that was! I did, and then happened upon some information that mentioned different types of clairvoyance depending upon what frequency the medium was tuned into. There was a form of clairvoyance that meant you could see things in the 3rd dimension or physical world. In the film 'Bruce Almighty' the lead character, Bruce, asked for a sign from God, and a truck full of road traffic signs pulled out in front of his car. He certainly got his sign but he did not see it.

Once I realised that I had this type of clairvoyance as well, I was flying, signs were everywhere, it was just superb. I would notice them on the side of white vans, on number plates and t-shirts, everywhere. I would hear things three times, and people would give me messages without even realising that they were doing it. I really began to tune into this frequency, and boy did my life change for the better. I had a communication method I trusted as back up, that worked in unison with my guides. It was great, even though a little bizarre.

It took about a year until I had a good substantial assortment of what I now see as my library of visual aids and divine messages. Working at this level meant that I was seeing miracles everyday, and my confidence levels grew and grew as a result.

One day I was driving home from my friend's. I had been for a treatment, I had been crying and was angry about how I had been treated and misjudged by certain people. My thymus or higher heart chakra had been open for a while but I felt it closing down because of the anger I was feeling. I even had a pain in my chest because of it. During my journey home a white van cut me up, so I had no choice but to see it and I noticed that the words written on the side, in big green letters said "Panic". Green is a colour associated with the heart chakra and I immediately knew I needed to do some work on healing my higher heart chakra to release the negative feelings that were crushing me. So when I arrived home I did a healing meditation and I could see an arrow piercing right through my heart, which was removed by my angels. This alleviated the pain immediately.

You might be thinking where did that arrow come from? Over the years I have removed what looked like arrows, swords, daggers, anchors, shackles, metal plates, hooks, chains, black symbols and an assortment of moving manifested energy from myself, my friends, and my clients. The one thing I have been guided to do is to not analyse where most of these things come from. The images are symbolic of negativity, and that's all I need to know. Some will have come from past lives, some from psychic attacks, even to the point of attacking ourselves and holding ourselves back, and some are astral inhibitors. My advice is to try not to over-analyse; you could end up paranoid. Just let it go and you'll be fine.

On another occasion I was in the process of buying my new property and I was driving home from my voluntary work at the local hospital. I asked my angels if there was anything else I needed to do when I got home other than the mental list I had already made. A bird flew straight across my windscreen; this is always a sign that a message is on the way from the Universe. Immediately after that I saw a white van with these letters on the side "BYBOXB48AM" I read it as Buy Box before 8am, which I saw as a reminder to call the estate agents with some urgent information they had requested before 8am the next morning. I thanked my angels and rang the estate agents as soon as I got home.

Another example was when I had more or less given up smoking, but one evening I asked my boyfriend to go and buy me a packet of cigarettes from the local shop. He was also able to read the 3rd dimensional signs, especially the ones on cars. When he came back he was excited at what he had seen outside the shop. There had been a car parked with a private number plate of NICOTX—what a blatant sign to give up smoking. It was still a while before I stopped smoking altogether. It took me seven attempts before I gave up, so stick at it if you are trying to kick the habit, as seven attempts is apparently the average. Smoking really damages your light as well as your health.

Other messages I got included hearing or seeing broken glass three times. If you notice this happening, check to see if you have been enclosed in a force field or glass box. It sounds crazy but it can happen. Blocks can develop way out in your aura and form a shield of energy, which can hold us back. I regularly check my aura is clear, right out to level 35, as egg-shaped clouds of contaminated energy can form and can cause problems. I once found a layer of muddy cloud-like energy around a lady outside of her God layer (layer 33) and, in order to clear it, I considered this cloud to be layer 34. I needed to surround it with the grid of light and that is why I use grids out to layer 35 now.

Alarms going off in the street or sirens are always a sign that something negative is around either me or my client, and this usually means a tie-cutting or space clearing needs to be carried out. Dripping taps and leaks mean unshed tears; flat tyres mean you are a bit deflated—with me the left tyres mean emotionally, and the right physically. If there is low frequency energy in my home, which can come through via TV or visitors, light bulbs will blow, and if that happens I clear the space immediately. Unless you ban all of the sex and violence on TV or on computer games, stop people coming into your home and live like a monk, it is virtually impossible to keep the lower frequency energy out of your space, so it is important to cleanse your home on a regular basis. The technique I have given previously can be used on your home and your garden. I advise you to take the grid to the boundaries of your property.

If a bird or butterfly flies close to you it means that a message is on the way from the Universe, so be aware of any guidance you feel you are getting, although it can take a while to learn to read and notice these 3D signs. I recommend watching the film 'Bruce Almighty'. It is a very clever film, full of important messages about using and abusing your power and being responsible. Children will love it too; it is really funny. As we raise our vibration, we become more and more powerful, and it is important to know that with greater power comes greater responsibility and greater karmic consequences.

There have been times when I have had my Brow chakra (third eye) blocked by outside influences. The sign for this is sunglasses when there is no sunshine, as the dark glasses just catch your attention, or I notice headbands and blindfolds. The blocks can look like sink plugs, metal bands or material tied around my head. When I meditate and see what is blocking my third eye, I visualise my angels taking it away. It is important that you visualise it being removed, in order to clear it.

Once again, I do not analyse where it came from, or if it's someone's fault, as it is usually to do with the energy attached to them, and without their knowledge. Even a family member or your dearest best friend can have something negative attached to them. Usually I will notice a change in mood when someone has something attached to them. People get entities attached to them regularly (you can pick them up in the supermarket) and a tie-cutting usually removes most things easily. Entities are just like fleas and are attracted to clean people, so if you have one, don't take it personally. Just remove it using the technique described earlier.

My usual warning for the presence of general rubbish is the two colours red and black. I can be driving along and my eyes will be drawn to someone wearing red and black. Black is the sign for something more sinister, such as entities or negative spirit attachments. If they are to my left it means that my energy needs cleansing or there is lower octane stuff at my destination. If it is on my right, it means that it is connected to someone else, perhaps someone I am thinking of, or the person I am on my way to visit.

You may be thinking, okay, but there is red and black all over the place. That's true, but for me it's the ones that stand out, its people who draw your attention, or you feel like you have had a tap on the shoulder. You will know when it happens. When I hear the word red or scarlet, it usually means *"Stop"*. If I am in a car and a red car cuts me up, it reminds me to change what I am thinking about, or to stop what I am about to do. If I see a picture or hear the name of the same animal three times in the day, it means I need to invoke that animal and pull in its energy to help me. As we saw earlier, they all mean different things, and the animal kingdom is there to help in spirit.

If you see red and black, please don't panic; they are just my sign to clear energy and it's become a daily part of my life now. These signs are from my library; yours could be different altogether.

On one holiday I visited a lovely 5 star hotel spa for a massage; we were treated like royalty. For a couple of days later after this massage I had stomach problems and began to feel really uncomfortable and bloated. I was in a supermarket and asked my guides what was causing it. My eyes were then directed to a shelf that had three bottles with cobras on the labels. I had removed lots of snake-type energies from clients, and I knew that this was what I needed to do to myself back at the hotel. I asked my higher self where this had come from, and I was directed to a label that said Cleopatra. It was then I realised that I had picked this bad energy up in the spa; its name was the Cleopatra Spa. I soon removed it, using a Crystal Ki net of light and my stomach settled immediately.

In early 2008 I was feeling particularly stressed with certain global transitional problems and I called out loud in frustration as I was driving my car home, *"Why did God choose me for this particular job?"* Seconds later a huge fruit and vegetable lorry passed with words on the side saying 'Well

Picked.' That really made me laugh and I felt so much better. God really does work in mysterious ways.

Basically, reading the 3rd dimensional signs is a very personal thing, and whilst anything you see or hear three times is a sign from the Universe, try to take notice of things you see on the side of vans. It could help you on your journey. I am very grateful for my 3D signs and messages, but my intuition is really good now, and I am also guided by spirit.

36. *Television and Radio*

As you develop spiritually, your chakras will become more sensitive as a higher frequency of light is present in your body. Once you have stimulated your chakras and activated your DNA changes, you have become a higher density light being, and this means that you need to take care of these chakras and your aura by keeping them clear of lower vibrational energy; cleaning your energetic body will become like cleaning your teeth—a matter of routine.

Performing regular space clearing on your home will be just as important. Everything electrical allows energy into your home. That means your TV, telephone, electrical appliances, computer and so on. These objects can also act as portals, allowing darker energies into your home, and it is therefore important to clear it on a regular basis.

You may be clairsentient and able to pick up the vibes, but if not there is no need to worry, as by using the space clearing technique in this book you can clear your whole house or your place of work in minutes. Remember to do your place of work at night, when no one is in the building.

The old-fashioned way of clearing was to burn sage and herbs, but I find the net of light works for me and it doesn't run the risk of burning my carpet or smelling as bad as burning sage. Playing some classical music and opening the windows regularly will always help too.

Many of these lower energies enter our home via the television, and the energy they attract is the same low frequency. This is why a lot of people who sit in front of the television, day and night, become docile and depressed. They really need to go outside to get some fresh air in order to clear that negative energy away and clear their minds. I believe TV is a form of mind-control wrapped in a pretty box, and can damage the sub-conscious. Watching sex, violence, horror movies and worst of all the news, which is full of doom and gloom, creates anger and sadness in the viewer. I've heard that in America, the average child has seen over 12,000 murders on TV and Cable TV by the time they are fourteen years old. We allow TV to pollute children's minds and then we are surprised and shocked when they are violent as a result. It's crazy.

We are highly influenced by what we see, and can be polluted by what we witness. For example, although the conscious mind knows that this may just be a movie you're watching, the subconscious mind will simply record it as violence, and will store that negativity without differentiating between the conscious and subconscious reality; it is then no longer just a fictional story on screen, as your subconscious mind just recalls the violence as normal behaviour.

Too much negative input not only damages your soul, but it damages your children too. Your soul is like an innocent child; why would you want to damage your soul in this way?

So, if you find yourself in a situation where you are watching something that you believe is damaging in this way, why not turn over to another channel, or better still, switch off altogether and go and do something healthy and fun instead.

We become what we think about most of all, and our thoughts create our experiences. If we think about negative collective mindsets, which attract more of the same, gradually accumulating into a huge mass of low frequency energy, we will realise that, collectively, we are making the planet a lower frequency than it should be. The whole world becomes affected by lower energies. So, if you must watch TV, try and watch pre-recorded films, where you can choose what to watch, and be assured that the content is less damaging than live television.

It is also worth considering that people who keep their children locked indoors, stuck in front of a television or computer screen, thinking they are keeping them safe from the dangers outside, are probably causing them more harm; it would be healthier for them to go out riding a bike, playing in the fresh air and getting some exercise. So many children look pale and over-weight due to their unhealthy lifestyles. I ask Archangel Michael to guide and protect my son when he goes out and then I just have faith that he will be safe. If you fear for your children, you send that energy into their lives, and can cause them more harm than good by worrying about them.

A friend's young son is addicted to playing computer games. He is as white as a ghost and always complaining, as these games are causing him so much harm and distress. His parents cannot see it. The games he plays are always making him feel inadequate because he cannot always reach the next level. He can become aggressive and sometimes violent when his parents try to turn the games off at bedtime. This is just terrible and I feel it is important that the general public should be constantly warned against the prolonged use of playing computer games. The warnings at present are not sufficient.

I also feel the same way about children using mobile phones. Its killing them with kindness in my opinion, and buying them expensive phones is madness. You may as well buy them a t-shirt which says *"Come and mug me, please"* in huge letters. Apart from that, cell phones emit radiation into our brains. This is especially damaging for young children, particularly those under the age of 10 years old. Parents should investigate further before handing out these dangerous gifts.

37. Developing Spiritual Growth

There are many ways to develop spiritual growth—spending time alone, reading, maybe listening to some e-books or CDs, having a really good look at yourself, and looking in the mirror of consciousness, because what is going on around you is a reflection of what is going on inside of you. So if you are experiencing bad things in your life, maybe you need to take a look deep within yourself and see what is going on and to get some help to repair the damage because, 'As within so without.'

I once went on a three day retreat, which really helped me move forward. Before then I never really considered myself to be a teacher, but after this experience I realised that teaching at a spiritual and energetic level is something I could do. I found out that my strengths were helping others to look at the bigger picture, to open their minds and just see the vastness of it all. To help people to realise, we are the painter, the paint and the canvas.

I had gone with a friend, and by the end of the first day we seemed to have attracted a small group of people who came together and connected with us, because they wanted to talk to us, or we would pick up on information that they needed intuitively. This group inspired me to teach my first workshop.

When I run workshops, teaching tie-cutting and space clearing, for example, I do try to raise the level of consciousness in the group I am teaching. We look at everything, not just removing negative energies from our space or negative spirit release, but also information relating to the bigger picture. I talk about why we have so many holistic healing therapies these days and why we need to make good use of them. I make the group aware that we need to cleanse both ourselves and the planet.

We talk about soul refinement, and working towards the ascension process of the whole planet. When my students leave, they go away a bit more enlightened and I get a great sense of satisfaction, which I could not really find in doing anything else.

I have come across some interesting books on my path. I am always looking on the internet to see what I can find and asking for the Divine Truth so that I find the right information, and more often than not that has been what I have found.

I am always learning something. I enjoy learning and even if I do not understand things with my conscious mind, I know that my soul understands it all. Feeding your soul is the way forward, and hopefully this book will help you too. I do question everything, and I am not easily misled by any means. I use meditation daily to speak to my guides and my higher consciousness so I am a lot happier and willing to put these words out into the world, whereas before I was still not quite sure if I should really be doing this, even though I kept hearing the words book, book, book, and ink, ink, ink, which was the Universe guiding me to do it.

I have not stopped writing since and things do change. This book is only my perception at a certain point in my journey. There are many other ways to grow and develop, and you need to find the one that suits you best, or use a combination of teachings and information.

Whenever there are planetary changes occurring, like Mother Earth's chakras being activated, I usually get together with a few friends and we meditate to help with these changes. One day, in town, I saw the words *"stop naked"* and I knew that it was a message for me to be celibate for a while before a particular meditation; the vital energy emitted when you climax may actually weaken your spiritual, creative power.

One way to still retain your power is to visualise the energy going from you into your partner, up their spine through their heart and into yours; take it in a figure of eight up through your spine out through the top of your head and into their crown, down through their head, their spine, then their heart through to your heart and back down your spine into your sacral. Just set the intention and visualise it happening. This will result in you not losing your vital life force. I remember watching a TV program about Chinese emperors, which stated that they did not allow themselves to climax during intercourse because they lost energy (Chi) and hence spiritual power as a result.

Since becoming a therapist, I have met many women who ask me about improving their sex lives and my first piece of advice is to suggest they call it making love. Then elevate that to spiritual love-making by asking their inner goddess to be totally present within them during the act of making love, and to connect to their partner's inner god.

The same goes for men of course, only they need to ask their inner god to be present and to connect with their partner's inner goddess.

This simple action can have amazing results, and is guaranteed to improve intimacy levels.

38. *Divine Truth and Prayer*

I like to start my day by giving thanks for the peaceful night's sleep I have had. I also like to state that I am a channel of love and light in order that

I do not use my own energy when working on people. I ask God to place a one metre wide orb of protective light around my Earth Star chakra to act as a filter for energies coming up from the earth, and request that it is camouflaged to protect it. I also ask for this protective orb to be placed around my son's Earth Star chakra.

I ask God to guide and protect me to ensure that all energies, entities and information I receive come from the Divine and from no other. I ask God to bless my home and family. Then I give my day to God and the Angels and let it all go. Having lit a candle I am ready to do my morning clearing and meditation session, after which I close all of my chakras both front and back and ask my higher self to choose the protection I need for my physical body if I am going out. Usually it is a layer of light and a layer of camouflage on each level.

I have heard many spiritual teachers say to their students *"go out and shine your light,"* however I feel guided to camouflage mine and I notice that if I don't, people tend to stare at me in the street. It also keeps the 'moths' away, so to speak, as they are very attracted to the light and have helped themselves to my energy in the past, so I now keep it under wraps, and I suggest you do the same.

At night I say thank you for the abundance in my life, I visualise my chakras being locked, and a special sleep pod forming around me, which is also camouflaged on the outside. I ask my Guardian Angel to watch over my physical body while I sleep and I say the following affirmation …

Affirm … *"I command that while my body sleeps my astral body will travel only to the higher planes of divine light, so be it and so it is."*

This allows me to bridge the lower planes where all of the lower energies are. When we are asleep at night we astral project (go out of body) and it is important to protect your physical body from nosey spirits and negative energies that can arise, by asking your Guardian Angel to keep watch over it for you.

I then finish with this prayer …

Prayer … *"Dear God, I ask to see, hear, know, think and feel the Divine Truth, to sense beyond all illusion and delusion. I ask God and the angels to remove all doubts and fears from my mind, body and soul as I sleep; I give thanks for my life and all life, Amen."*

Once this is done I feel content to go to sleep and have noticed that if I forget, I have a restless night and problems can occur as a result.

I feel that asking for the Divine Truth is important; many books and gurus advise us to seek the truth. The wording is critical as there is a difference between the truth and the divine truth. Consider this: if you have ten people all from similar backgrounds and you sit them in front of a movie and ask them to write a page about the film's true meaning, I can assure you what you will get are ten different versions of how they perceived the film's truth to be. As each person's truth will be dependent on where they are in their life journey, the unhappy people will write about the negative aspects in the movie, and the positive people will write about the positive aspects. They are all the truth, but only from their own perception, and hence, not the Divine Truth. The Divine Truth is God's version, the enlightened version of Truth.

A lot of books are filled with their author's truth and perspective as it was at that point in their life journey. These are ego-based in general. That is why I wanted to wait until now to write this book. Although I do have an ego, I have transcended many levels of ego, and that keeps me human, but I am very enlightened and happy with the information I have written.

Spiritually I am now in a high level of consciousness and have been finding Divine Truths for years, and I am satisfied with my findings. Whilst I still have much to learn, I could not write these words if I did not believe them myself, but I still urge you to carry out your own search for Divine Truth. There is only one Divine Truth and when we find it, we attain self-realisation and start to prepare for the next step in our spiritual evolution through other planes of existence.

39. Universal Spiritual Laws

One of the most important things I have learned on my journey so far is about Universal Spiritual Laws. According to Diana Cooper's brilliant book, *A Little Light On Spiritual Laws,* there are 36 spiritual laws that govern all of life on Earth. I highly recommend this book, and will write about a few of my favourites as they have taught me so much about myself and the people around me. This book also contains vital information to help you learn about the mystery school we all live in; from how it all works as a mirror to teach us about our own shortcomings, to creating abundance, good karma and much more. This book is the first one I recommend my students to buy, as it has changed my life and it could change yours too. Here are just a few of my favourite laws.

The Law of Reflection

This explains that the Universe, and life as we know it, act a magic mirror, reflecting back at us the true aspects of ourselves that we need to address and improve—or not as the case may be. The outer world or reality reflects our life and what we need to learn about the shadow self. The people you like are mirroring aspects of yourself that are positive, and the people you don't like are mirroring the part of yourself that your soul is trying to bring to your attention. You will attract people to you that mirror your attributes, be they good or bad. Like attracts like. Look at the people you do not like and look at yourself. The mirror never lies. When you are aware, you can alter your negative behaviour to suit.

For example, if your lover is arrogant and maybe drinks too much alcohol, ask yourself *"Am I arrogant and do I drink too heavily?"* Is your child always in trouble at school? Are you behaving badly and is this is being reflected in your child's behaviour? Are your taps leaking or have you had a flood recently in your home? These things represent unshed tears and emotions that are being kept inside. These can lead to serious disease in the body. So get a good sad movie and cry, cry, cry. The tap will probably stop dripping. Mine did. Has everyone you bumped into today been angry? Maybe you need to deal with your own anger issues? If you notice people limping, maybe you need more balance in your life?

Do you see how it works? Everything we need to know is right there in front of us when we take notice and become more aware.

The Law of Attraction

This law is simple. We attract that which we think about most. The movie *The Secret* is all about this law. If you are a negative person, you will attract negative people and situations into your daily life. If you are the kind of person that talks about your friends behind their backs, don't be surprised when you find out they have been talking about you—your actions are being mirrored by them. Gossip is a very bad thing and causes a lot of pain. It is your fault, not theirs.

If you pick fault with yourself or see yourself as a victim you will attract people who will pick on you and act out the victimiser—you made yourself the victim. Change the way you look at things, and the things will change the way they look.

On the other hand, if you are a kind, positive person, you will attract similar attributes, and have a happy life. If you have a dream, you will attract people and situations that will help you to achieve that dream. One step at a time.

The Law of Projection

This law is about us projecting our beliefs onto other people. If you have a bad experience with a particular relationship for example, and you decide that therefore all men/women are bad and tell everyone this, you are projecting your belief onto others. You have created a negative belief system in your mind and are spreading wrong information. This can cause a lot of damage, as some people are very vulnerable and will believe the same. The result will be further spreading of negative information that will attract more bad partners to you and to those who believed your statement. We project our good and bad attributes onto other people by saying things like *"You must feel terrible about your ex,"* because we feel terrible and expect them to feel the same when it is not always the case. Statements like *"Everyone loves chocolate!"* and *"Everyone hates spiders!"* are, again, projections of beliefs. Both statements are incorrect.

When we fall in love, we project that love onto one another, and cannot see any shortcomings in the other person. As the relationship moves on we see deeper aspects of ourselves projected in the other and believe them to be their negative or positive attributes, but truly they are ours, not theirs. They are only acting as a mirror.

The Law of Resistance

This law is about pushing away things we really want. We do this by using words like don't, can't, won't, etc. The conscious mind can assimilate these negative words but the subconscious mind does not recognise them at all.

If you say *"Don't drop that cup"* to a child, the child's subconscious mind will hear *"Drop that cup."* It is better to say, *"Take care with that cup."* Use positive phrases and leave the negative words out. For example, we all say things like *"Don't forget to put the cat out please,"* to our partners. However, their subconscious mind will hear *"Forget to put the cat our please"* and come to bed leaving the cat to have a party. Changing the way we talk to one another is vital and in that instance a better phrase to use would be *"Remember to put the cat out please."*

We must leave out the negative connotations to master this law and saying things like *"I don't want to be single"* will keep you single. Concentrate on saying *"I would love to meet my soul mate"* and see how things change. We resist success by saying *"I can't stand this job."* We resist having a loving relationship by saying *"I am never going to meet the right person."* We resist being happy by saying *"I am so unhappy,"* and your statement creates your experience. It is possible to turn things around by saying more positive things like *"I am healthy, wealthy and wise,"* and therefore cover all areas.

The Law of Prayer

The law of Prayer is about asking for your desires, believing that they are on their way, and also showing gratitude for the blessings you do have.

It is also important to take steps towards what you hope to achieve when your request is granted. God listens to all prayers, and grants the ones that are from a pure heart and with good intentions, and so this is the best way to approach prayer.

Demanding, begging or cheating will not get you anywhere, God can read your mind and knows if you deserve or not, so always pray from a pure heart and with integrity. Start to make plans having faith that your prayer will be answered. This will also help your desires to manifest. Prayers that are for the highest good of all get to the front of the queue, so think about the bigger picture when you pray.

As I said, I am not a religious person but I do pray morning and night, giving thanks for the blessings in my life, usually when I am in bed. It is important to pray. God does not care where you pray, so long as you do. Remember to give thanks when you pray. We all have something to say thank you for, as we are all blessed in some way.

Now that you have read a few of the spiritual laws, maybe you can look at your relationship with your partner, or your family, work colleagues or friends, in a different light. The ones you don't like are teaching you the most by acting as a mirror of your negative aspects. They are your greatest teachers and you should honour their spirit for the lessons they are showing you. Change yourself and they will change with you, and you will attract people more akin to your lighter self. See yourself as happy and fulfilled and you will make your life change accordingly.

Many of us search for love and then we complain about our partners. Look again; are they a reflection of you? The trick is not to try to change them, but to change yourself. As we develop, it is sometimes necessary to move on and leave some people behind. They could be people who are bad for us, or even some of our dearest friends. This can be heart-breaking, but it is imperative that we cut ties and move on in order to fulfil our goals and dreams. The old saying that 'a rolling stone gathers no moss' comes to mind. Try to learn not to get too attached to people or things, as they are all only on loan from God, and can be gone in the blink of an eye. Practising detachment leads to a state of inner peace.

"Charaiveti, charaiveti," said Gautama Buddha: Keep on moving.

I have let many people go as they were not ready for change, and whilst it hurt terribly at the time, it was the best thing I ever did. The hurt does go away and I have met some of the most wonderful people on my new path, true soul mates. I am truly blessed and grateful.

40. Seed Atoms, Life and Death

Life does not spontaneously appear in the Universe. It is believed to be constructed by architectural celestial beings. Once the personality has been created, the Universal Sons, known as the Life Carriers, take that life to the designated planets. These Sons are divided into three groups: the Senior Life Carriers, the Assistant Life Carriers and the Custodians.

The life patterns and the personalities are created by God the Father, and God the Son. These are then brought to their home planet by the life carriers, and through them, the divine spark and living plasma are planted via the Mother Spirit. The vital spark gives life energy to the body and mind of the new being. These sparks are referred to as permanent Seed Atoms. These contain all of the required information about the new being, on a mental, astral and physical level. The life carriers place them in the womb at the point of conception.

Seed atoms contain the blueprint records and memory of everything needing to be done by that soul when it incarnated, with each seed atom containing its vibrational nature. Permanent seed atoms are also planted in sacred places in order to allow a portal of light to be anchored into the planet at that point.

When we die, the energetic bodies detach from the physical body, followed by the seed atoms, the mental, the astral and the physical. The consciousness of the soul awakens in the astral state and experiences that particular bardo. Bardo is a Tibetan word literally meaning 'intermediate state.'

When the physical seed atom is released after death, the silver cord breaks, recoils, and gets reinstated back into the skeletal system of the deceased. The mental is connected to the pineal, the emotional to the liver, and the physical to the heart.

Later, the light body is greeted by Angels and family members, who are all ready and waiting for the new arrival. My deceased nephew came to visit me during a meditation only six days after he died. He told me that his father (my brother, who died ten months before) and his uncle were waiting for him when he arrived, and that gave me a great sense of peace, as I knew he was happy and supported by these two people whom he loved very much.

I have always believed in life after death from as far back as when I was at school, and a girl in my class would tell me about the ghosts in her house. I just always had an inner knowing that there was something beyond what we call death, and that we were surrounded by spirit, but it was not something you could speak openly about in a catholic home. As a child I always had a feeling that someone was standing behind me, and to this day I am not sure whether it was my grandmother or my guardian angel, Jacob. Either way, I knew someone was there, and as a result I very rarely felt alone or afraid.

This has since led me to question what happens when we pass over. According to Dr Deepak Chopra and his comments on near-death experiences in his book *'Life after Death,'* he says that the following happens:

1. The physical body stops functioning. The dying person may not be aware of this, but eventually realises that this has occurred.
2. The physical world vanishes. This can happen by degrees; there can be a sense of floating upwards or of looking down upon familiar places as they recede.
3. The dying person suddenly feels lighter and freed of limitation.
4. The mind, and sometimes the senses, continue to operate; gradually however, what is perceived becomes non-physical.
5. A presence grows which is felt to be divine; this presence can be clothed in a light or in the body of Angels or Gods. It can also communicate to the dying person.
6. Personality and memory begin to fade but the sense of 'I' remains.
7. This 'I' has an overwhelming sense of moving on, to another phase of existence.

This seven-fold awakening is not the same as what people understand as going to heaven. Researchers often call this the inner-life phase, a transition between the mental states of being alive and the mental state of realising that one has passed on. There are many specifics that change from person to person. Not all near-death experiences go into the light; some people report travelling to various planets in space or to other worlds, according to their religious beliefs. Some experience a judgement scene, which can be quite harsh or hellish; however it can also be full of satisfaction.

According to the *'Tibetan Book of Living and Dying,'* we move through four bardos:

1. Life
2. Dying and death
3. After-death
4. Rebirth.

According to Tibetan Buddhism, these are the four interlinked realities of our entire existence. Buddhists believe that life and death are one whole; death being the beginning of another chapter of life, a continual cycle of evolution and growth, always in existence in one bardo or another, just living in different levels of consciousness.

When we cross from this 3D world to the spirit world we are in the field of Akasha, the etheric field of consciousness. This is real and all previous awareness of waking and dreaming are unreal. We take a quantum leap in our conscious awareness into the infinite realm of possibilities. It is believed that we are taken to where we need to be, according to our belief systems. Therefore if you are a Christian you will spend time in a dimension that suits those beliefs; likewise if you are a Buddhist or a Muslim, the dimension will suit your specific needs.

The next step, I believe, is that you work through any unfinished business or karma in your new world. When my nephew died I had a strong urge to practice a chant I had learnt to help purify his negative karma. The Tibetans use this six syllable chant *"Om Benza Satto Hung."* This is for healing and purification regarding the deceased. When we spoke, my nephew thanked me for doing this. I often use this chant during meditations to help the souls heal when I hear of a death or a natural disaster. Chanting can really help the deceased acquire a better future bardo.

My nephew was buried, but in most countries and religions, the body is cremated. The reason for this is because they view the dead person's corpse as holding their negative karma. When they are cremated their karma is transformed and transmuted, thus leading to a better reincarnation. The dead person is purified by the flame. Personally, I prefer the idea of cremation, mainly for the reason that is can be easier for the family.

My younger family life was hectic, my four older siblings and my nephew lived with my parents. There was always something going on with eight of us living in a three-bedroom terraced house. When I discovered that we choose most of the major experiences in our lives, our spiritual contracts, including our mother and father and so on before we incarnate, I must admit it changed my perception vastly. From that perspective, I can see why I chose my parents; they were both wise old souls who lived simple, quiet lives. My sisters were like chalk and cheese, completely different. My brothers were like my dad in many ways.

I was lucky, as my karma was good, but it must be a bitter pill to swallow for those who have experienced harsh, violent or abusive lives. Choosing an abusive parent to help you work through your karma must be difficult to accept; nevertheless, from the karmic perspective, that is the case and when you accept it, you can let go and move on. You chose it, the good, the bad and the ugly, in order to learn and grow.

Life on Earth is short and full of tests; it is a material existence. As we gain mastery of this world, having passed these tests, it is believed that we move into what are known as the Mansion Worlds, up to and through our solar system, constellation and Local Universe. Our spiritual development continues into the Super Universe where we are prepared for eventual transit to Havona. In the Havona worlds, we focus on intellectual, spiritual and experiential attainment where we are set tasks in order to attain higher levels of spiritual progression. The Havona worlds are training grounds, occupied by perfect beings. Understanding the make-up of these perfect worlds is presently beyond human comprehension but, needless to say, we will enjoy our time there. We do have leisure time on these worlds. It is not all about work.

When we have passed through these worlds, it is time for our most important sleep ever, as we are prepared for our transition to the paradise that awaits us. The last transition sleep graduates a Soul into the realm of the eternal; it is a transition from one state of being to another. When we awake we are guided by beings assigned to take us to Paradise. Our arrival in Paradise signifies that we have found God, we are home.

Death is only the beginning of an eternal journey and fantastic voyage of discovery. According to the book of Urantia, God is a multi-faceted being, consisting not only of God The Father, God The Son, and God the Holy Spirit but many other aspects too. In general, when we think of God we tend to think of one Divine Being, in a singular sense. The Book of Urantia will open your mind and consciousness, and set out an explanation of creation to you in its infinite and absolute levels, talking about not only this Universe, but also the Super Universe, the seven Super Universes, Paradise Trinity and much more.

It explains fully the different aspects of God, the hierarchy, and all of the other beings in existence, from Angels and Galactic Masters to Thought Controllers and Time Lords. There are many beings in charge of each sector and Universe, from The Ancient of Days, the Faithful of Days, to the Divine Councillors and even Beings in charge of Paradise Trinity.

According to the Book of Urantia, the numbers of planets habited and uninhabited in all of these Universes are far beyond the human comprehension of numbers. There are billions and trillions of these planets out there, much too far away for our current, limited, scientific technology to discover.

41. Summary

The world is changing; mankind and the whole planet are evolving into higher levels of consciousness and a purer way of being. Apparently, at 11.11am on 21st December 2012 we may see the results of these changes, both globally and universally. Until then, no one really knows exactly what is going to happen. I believe that there will be a phenomenal change in consciousness and, depending on our spiritual attainment, our individual perception may change the hologram we call reality, potentially allowing us to live in a state of peace and harmony, free from the lower frequency energies that temporarily pollute our planet.

There are many ways to help cope with the changes taking place, but none of us can avoid the process. There are many things we can do to help purify both ourselves and the planet, such as asking God to bless our food and water. Blessing it yourself uses your valuable energy; asking God to bless it uses Source energy, allowing you to conserve yours. Every time it rains, I ask God to put sea salt into each drop of rain on the planet so as to cleanse the atmosphere, the earth and the waterways all over the world.

Try to focus your mind on the good things in life and don't give your power to the darkness by thinking about it too much, if at all. Believe it or not, most of the destruction we see in the news is all part of the cleansing process on a global level, and is part of the Divine Plan. Sometimes we need to go backwards in order to move forwards.

It is important to heal our own shadow self by receiving some form a complementary therapy, and/or practising meditation and prayer. We also need to develop as spiritual beings, in order to cope with the changes.

All of these simple things have a large effect and make a big difference, so ask God to bless you, your family and all life on Earth. There is no need to push people to change; we are all waking up in accordance with divine will, so it is important to be patient with our fellow man. It is sometimes difficult not to get frustrated with our friends and families when we seem to be awake and they appear to be still asleep, confined to the 3rd dimension, but they will catch up. God is in charge of everyone's awakening.

The main thing to remember is that we are moving towards a new way of life, a perfect way of living and being. The Divine Plan is manifesting and will continue to do so until permanent change has occurred and we have evolved to higher levels of consciousness. This change is not just global; it is universal.

I hope you enjoy the trip and may God bless us all.

42. Bibliography

Everything you always wanted to know about your body but so far nobody's been able to tell you.
Chris Thomas & Diane Baker

Life after Death
Deepak Chopra

The Divine Matrix
Gregg Braden

A Little Light on Spiritual Laws
Discover Atlantis
Diana Cooper

The Mystery of the Crystal Skulls
Chris Morton and Ceri Louise Thomas

The Secret (I think the DVD is better than the book)
Rhonda Byrne

The Only Planet of Choice - Essential Briefings from Deep Space
Phyllis V. Schlemmer & Mary Bennett

Healing ADD - The Breakthrough Program That Allows You to See and Heal the 6 Types of ADD (A must read if your child has ADD)
Daniel G. Amen, M.D.

The Urantia Book
The Urantia Foundation

Crystal Ki Workshops,
Treatments and Products

Vibrational Body Care products for men and women,
Books, CD's and Downloads.

Crystal Ki Workshops from Beginner to Advanced levels
Please visit our web site for details of other workshops

To book Janine Regan-Sinclair to speak at your event
or to arrange a press interview, contact:
info@thecrystalkifoundation.com

www.crystalki.com

www.thecrystalkifoundation.com

LOVE